This Book

Happy Easter!

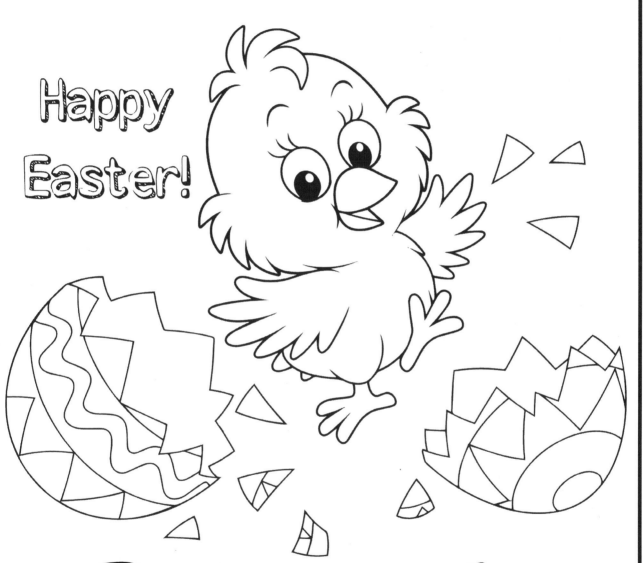

Belongs To

∩∩∩∩∩∩∩∩∩∩∩∩

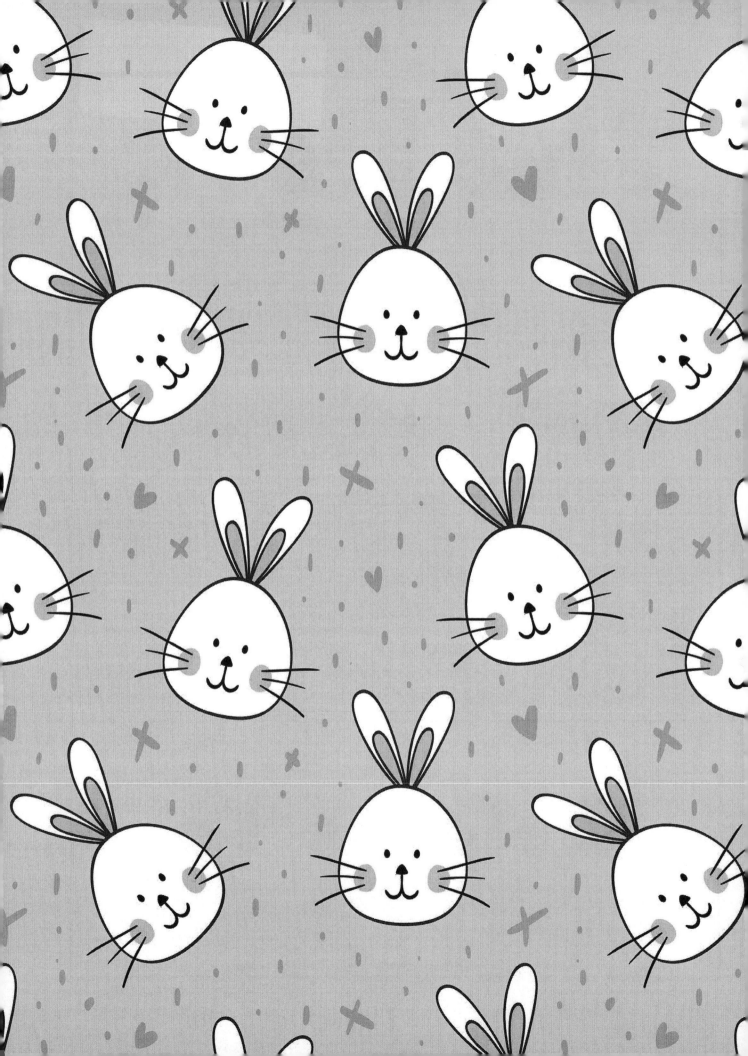

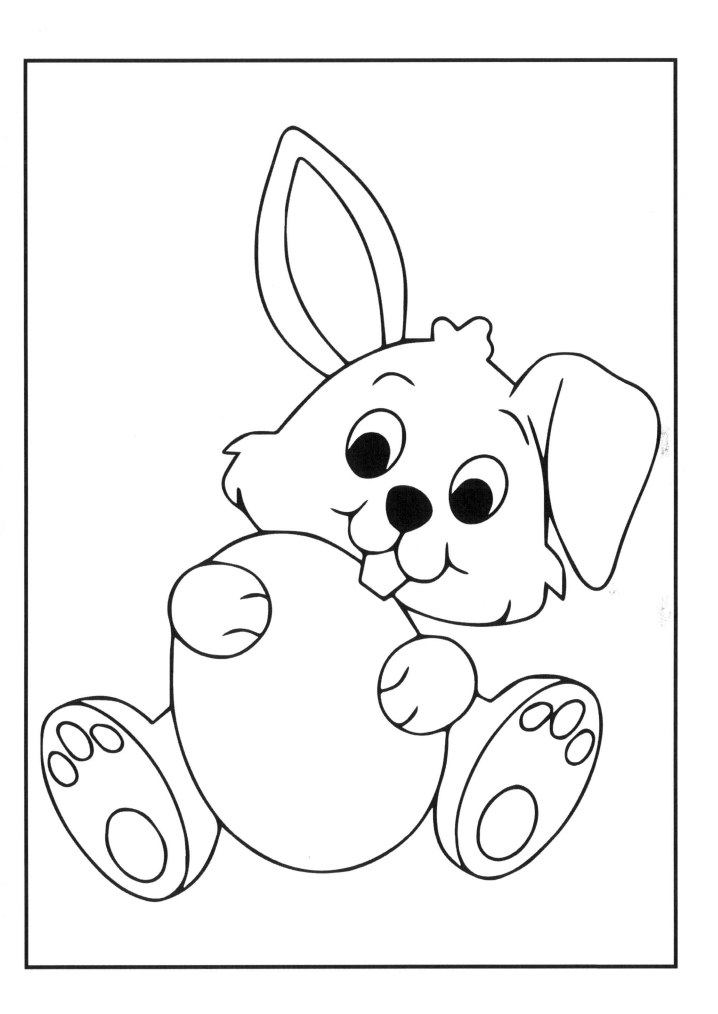

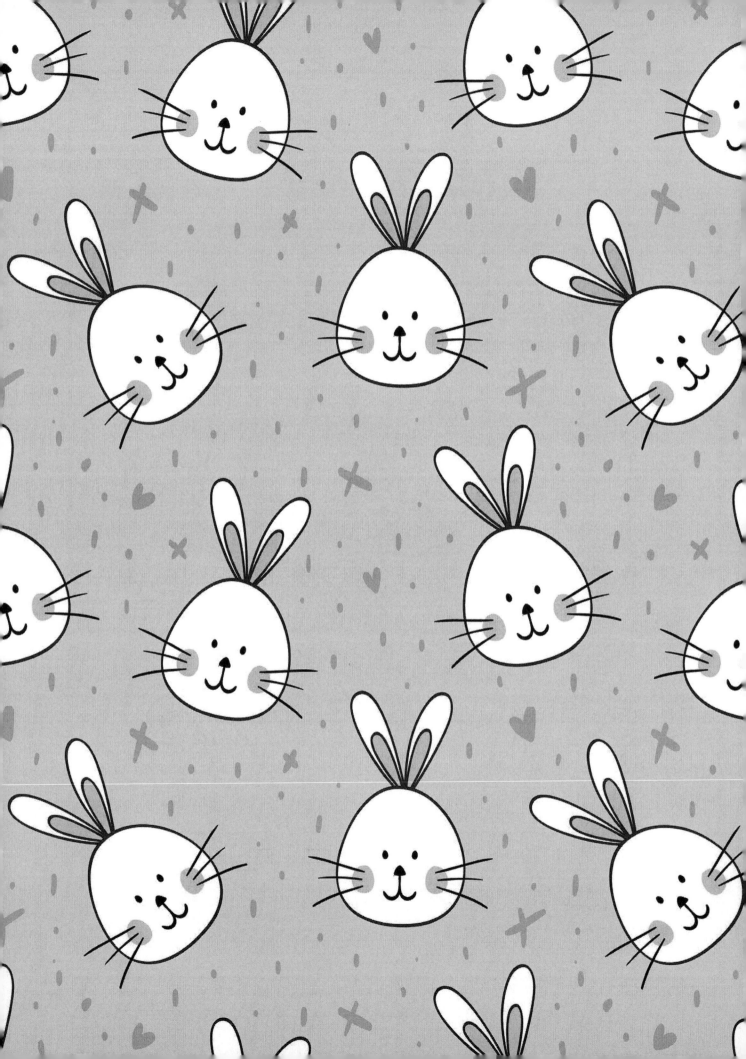

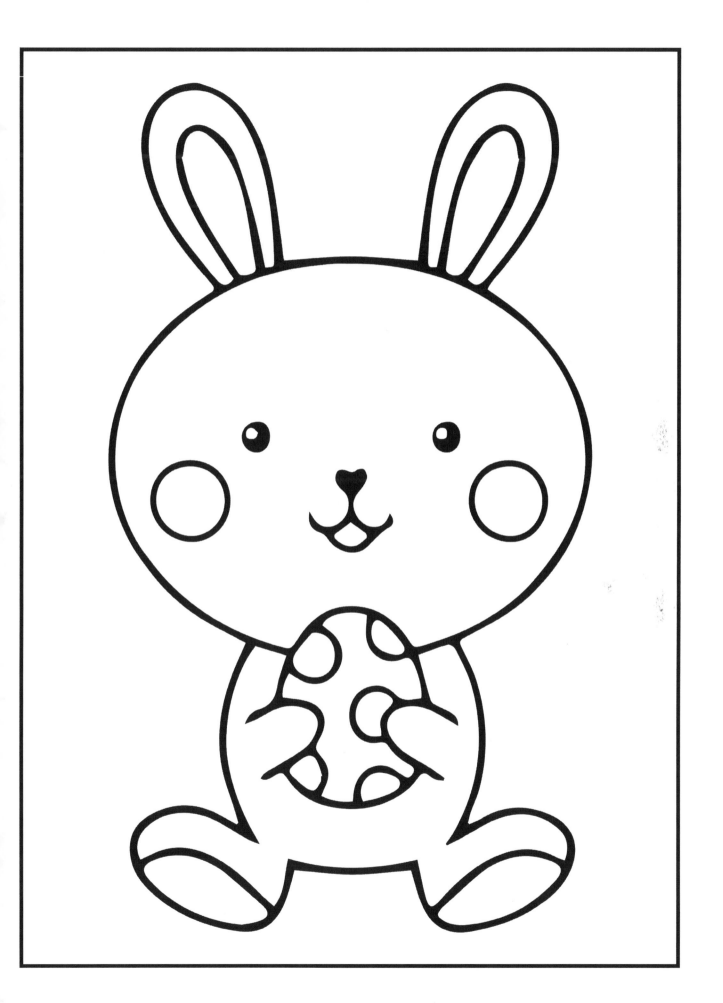

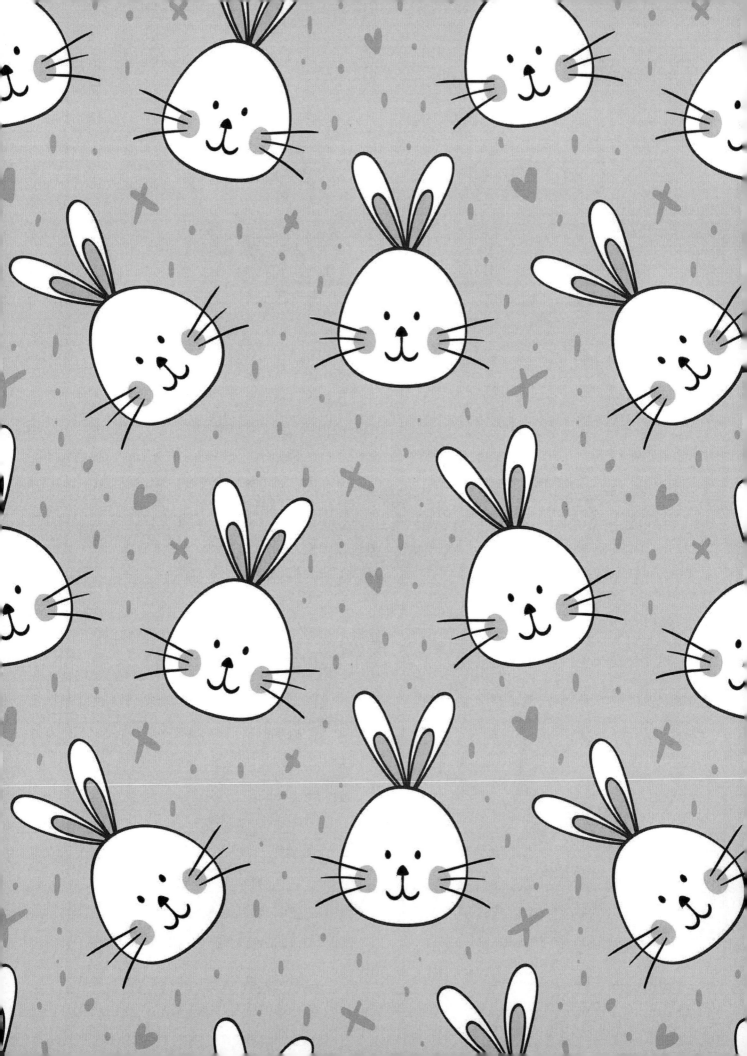

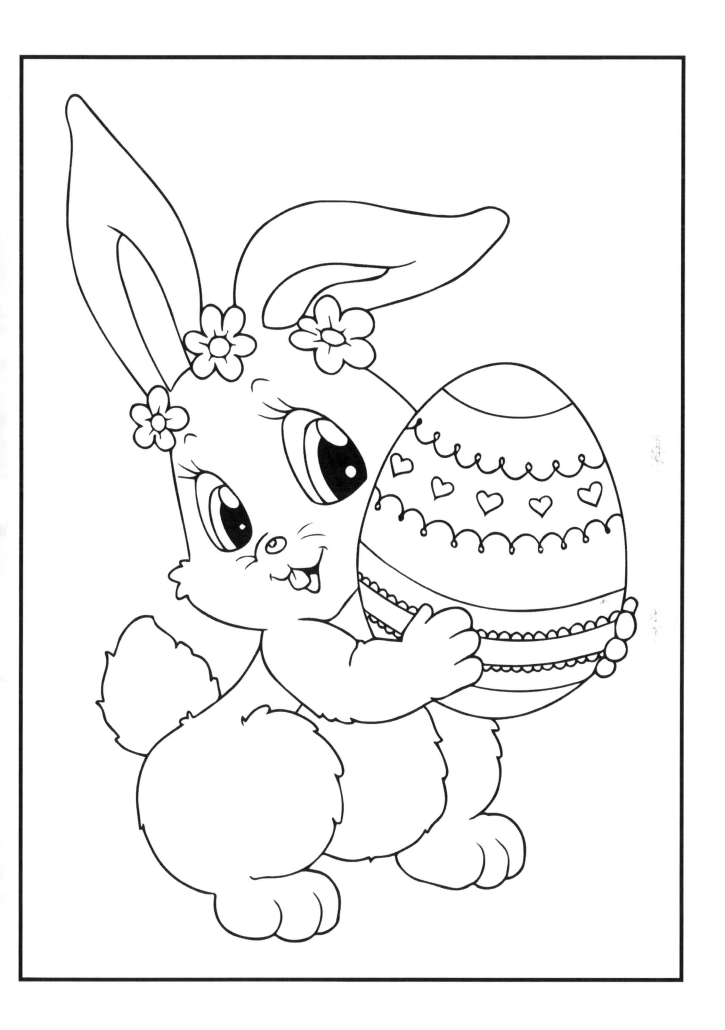

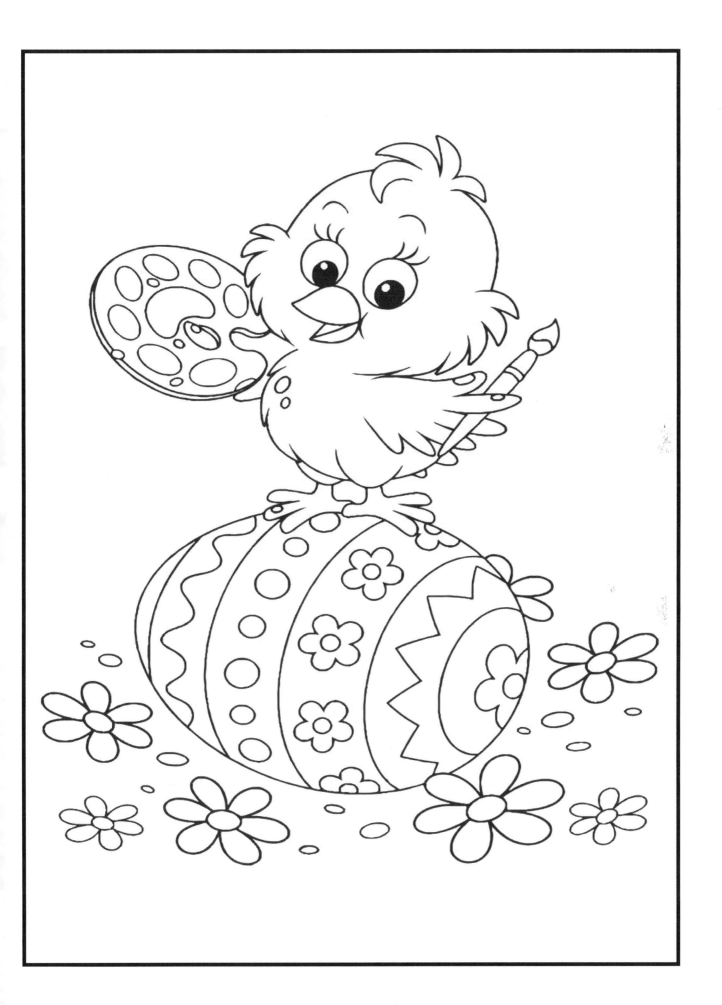

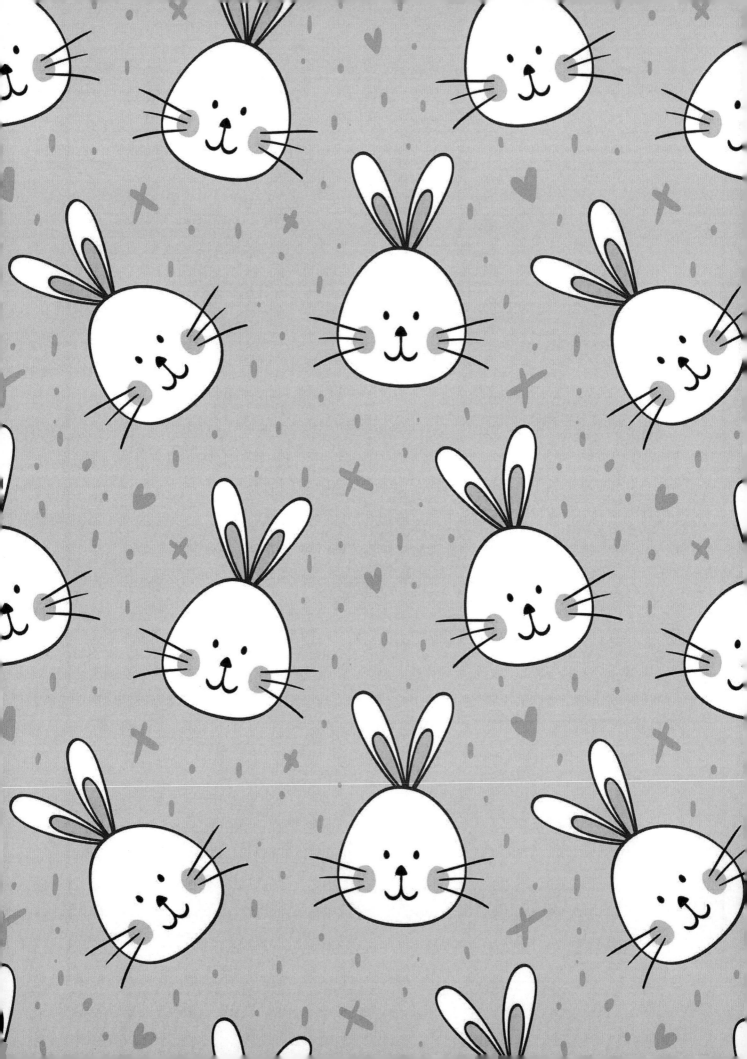

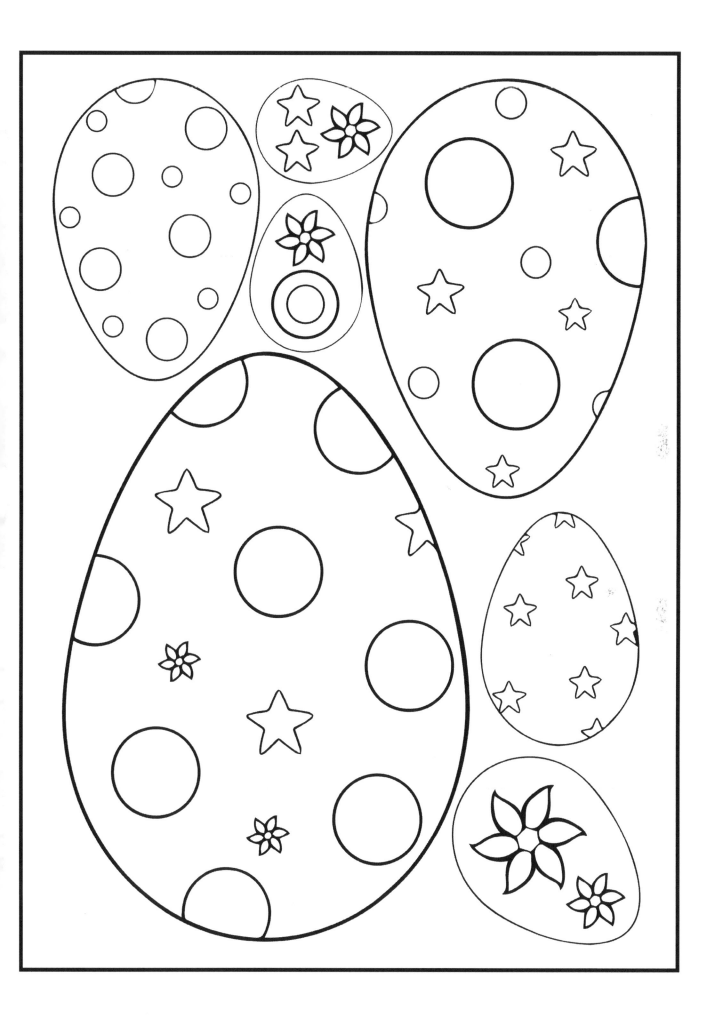

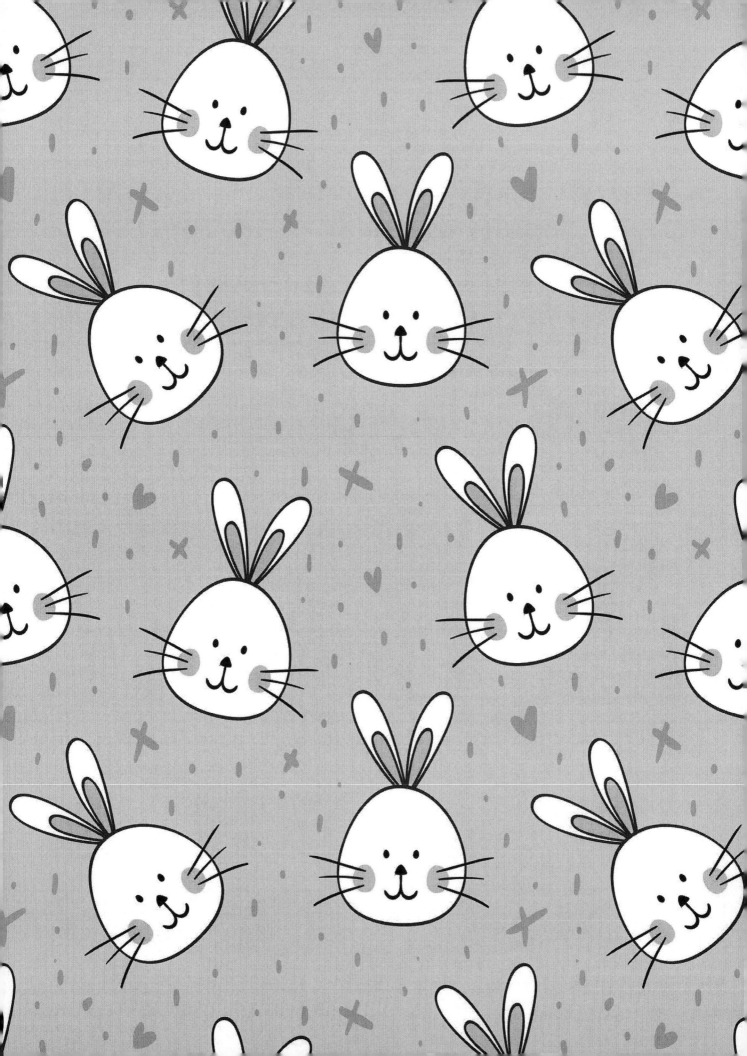

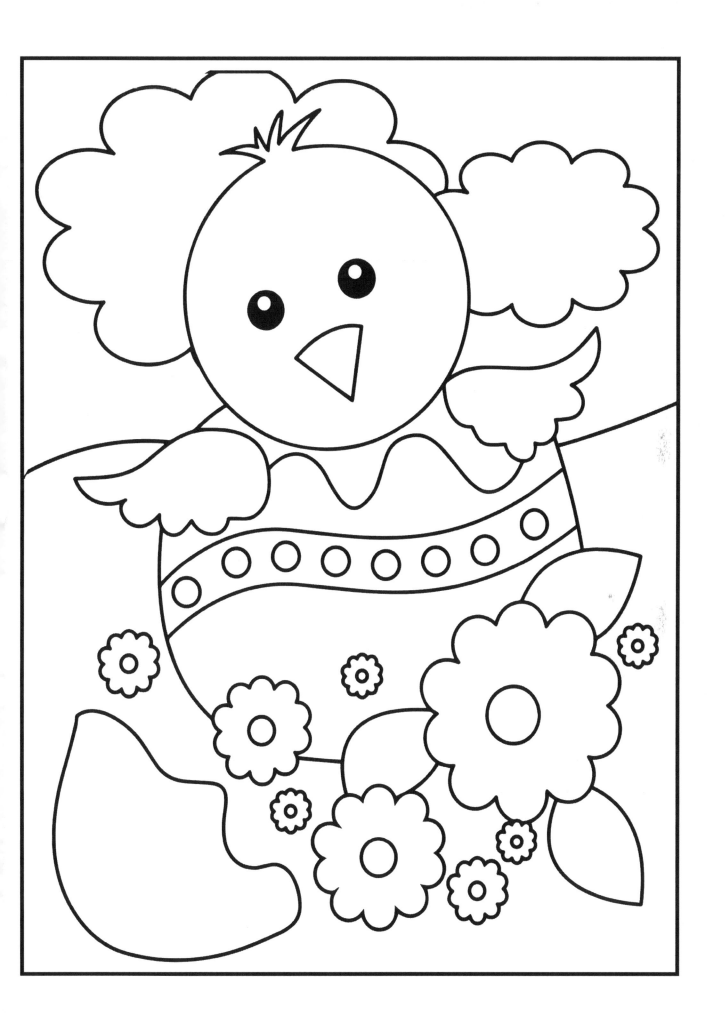

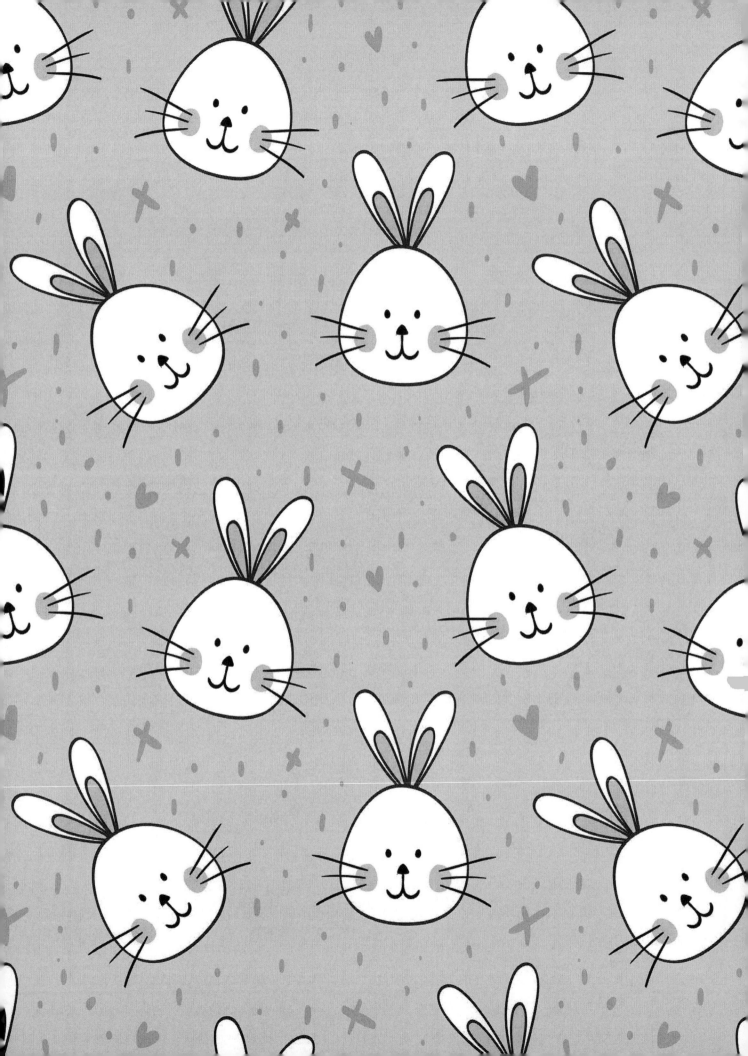

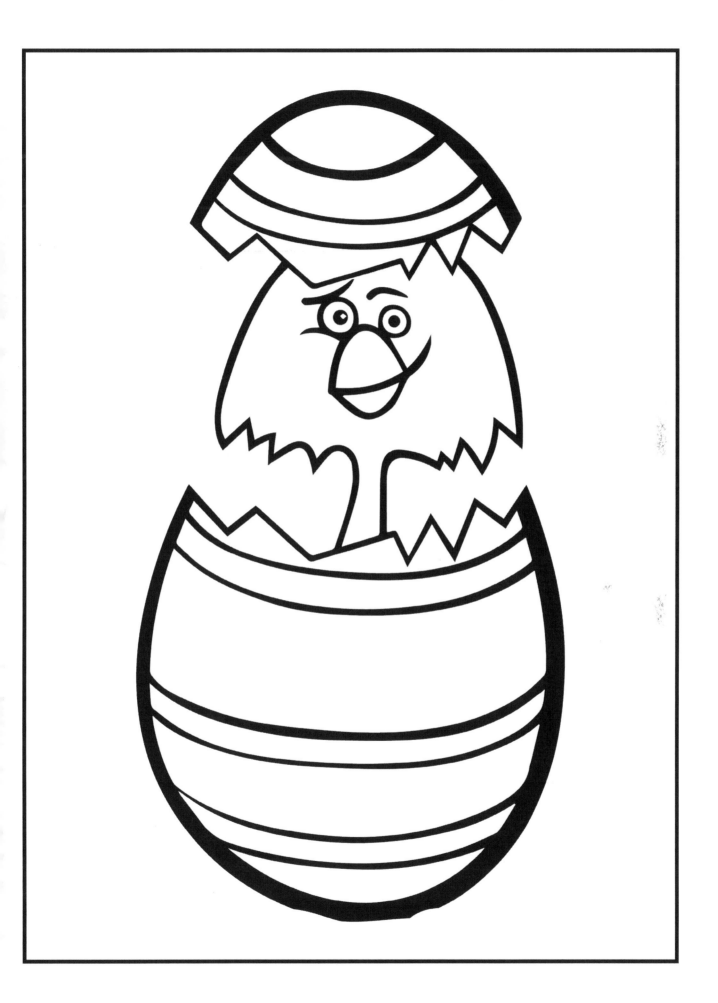

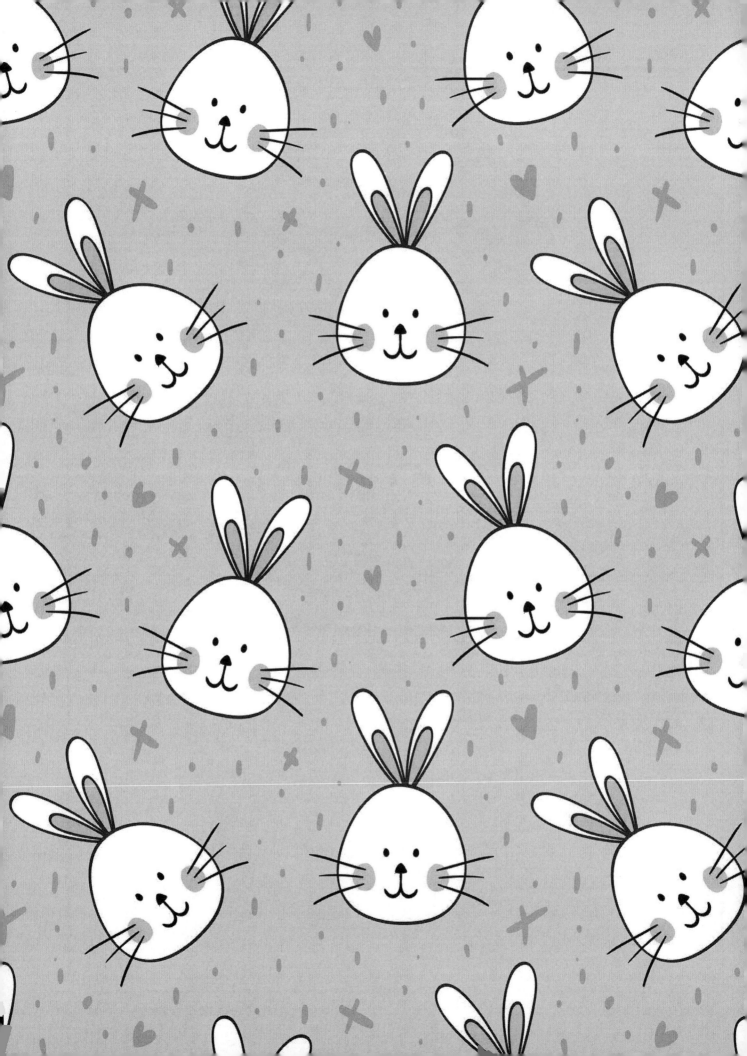

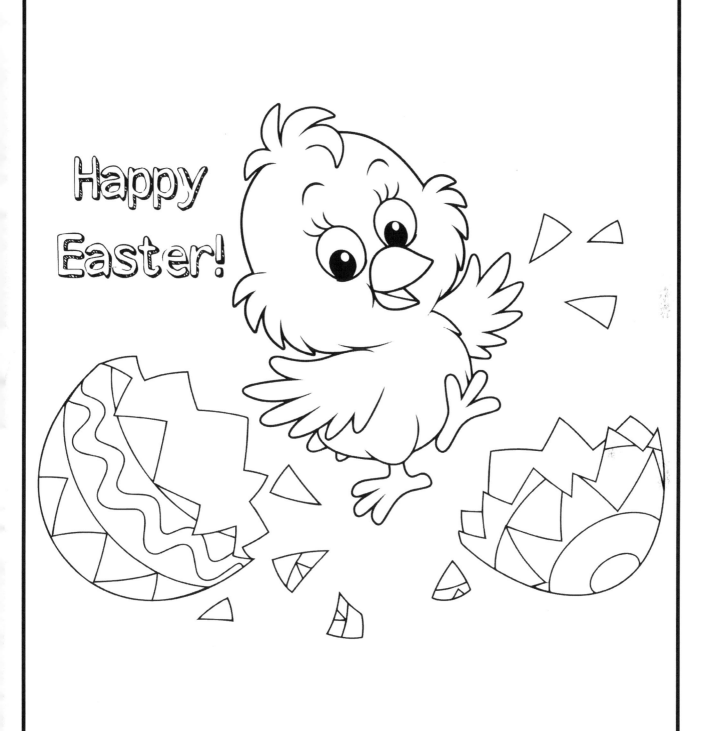

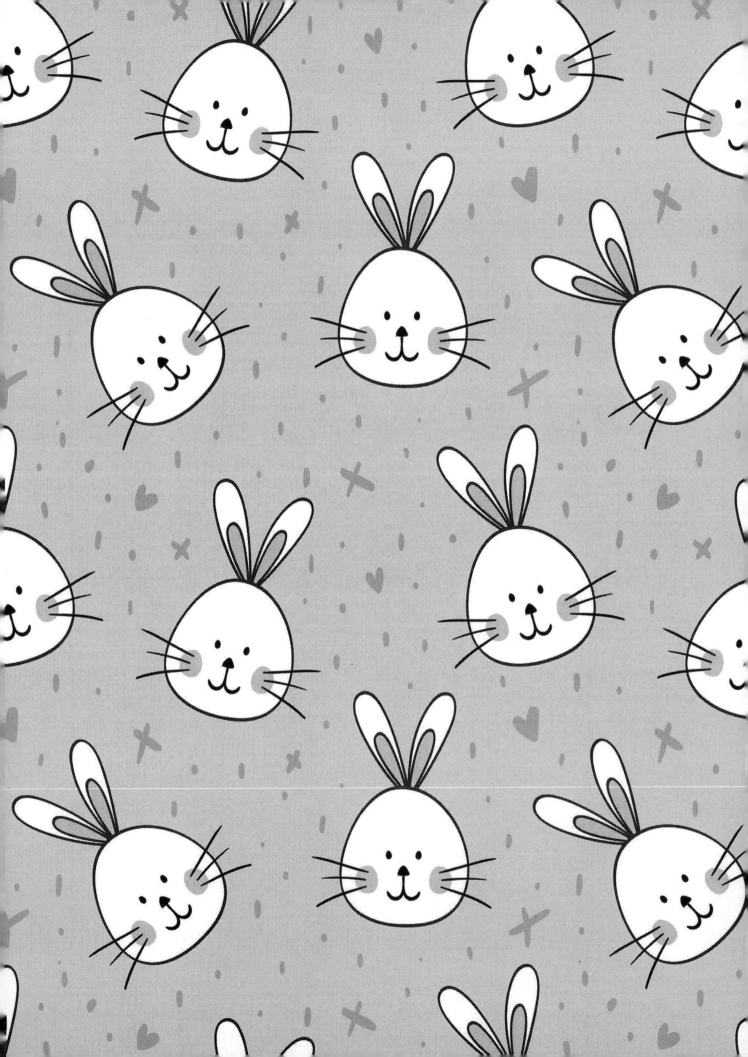

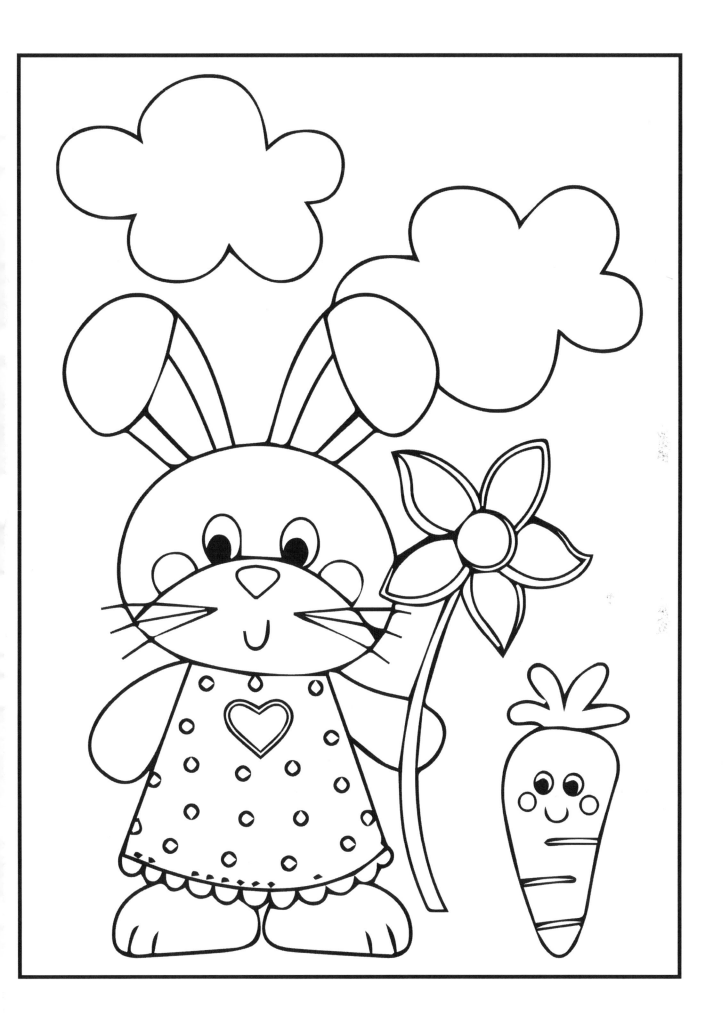

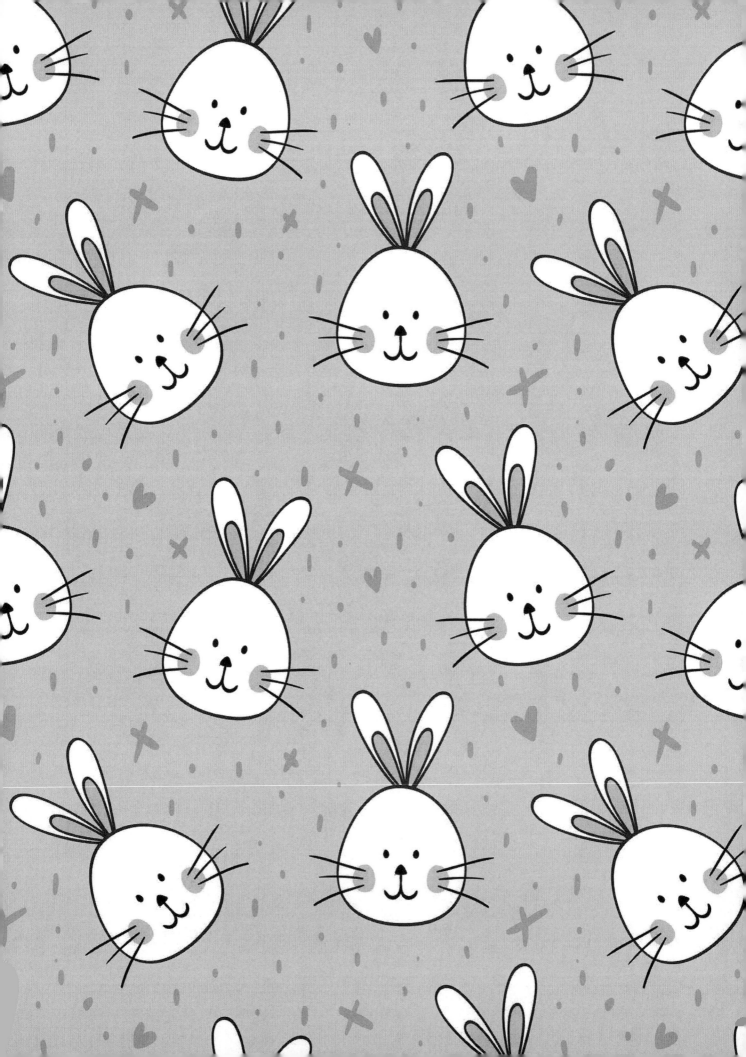

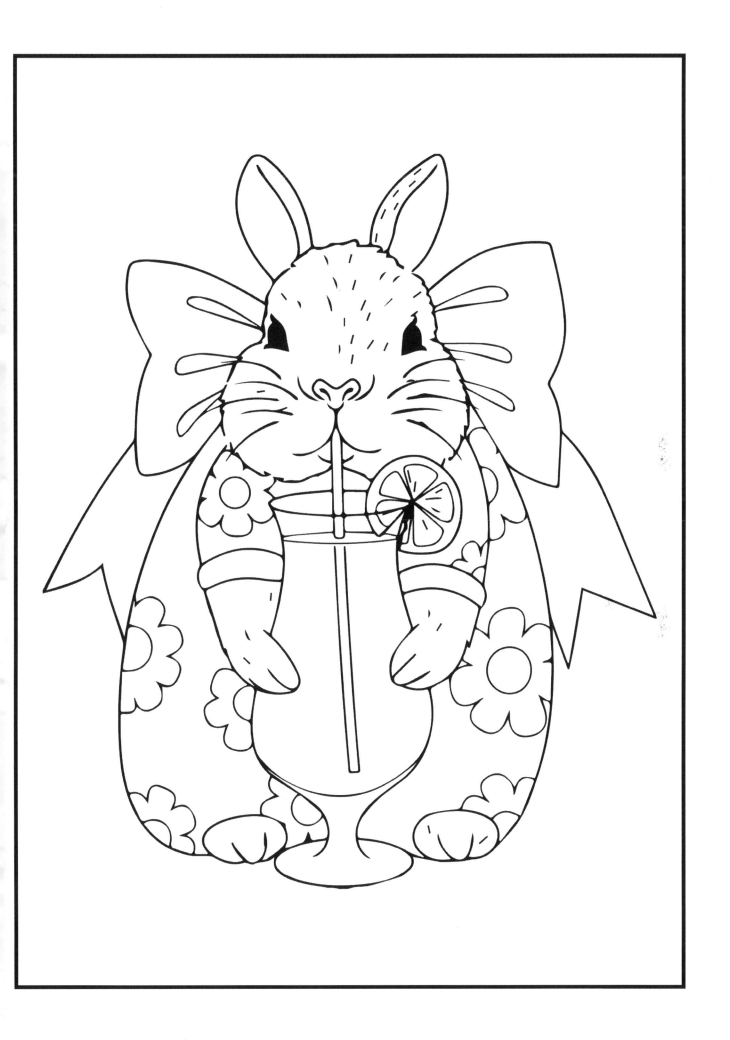

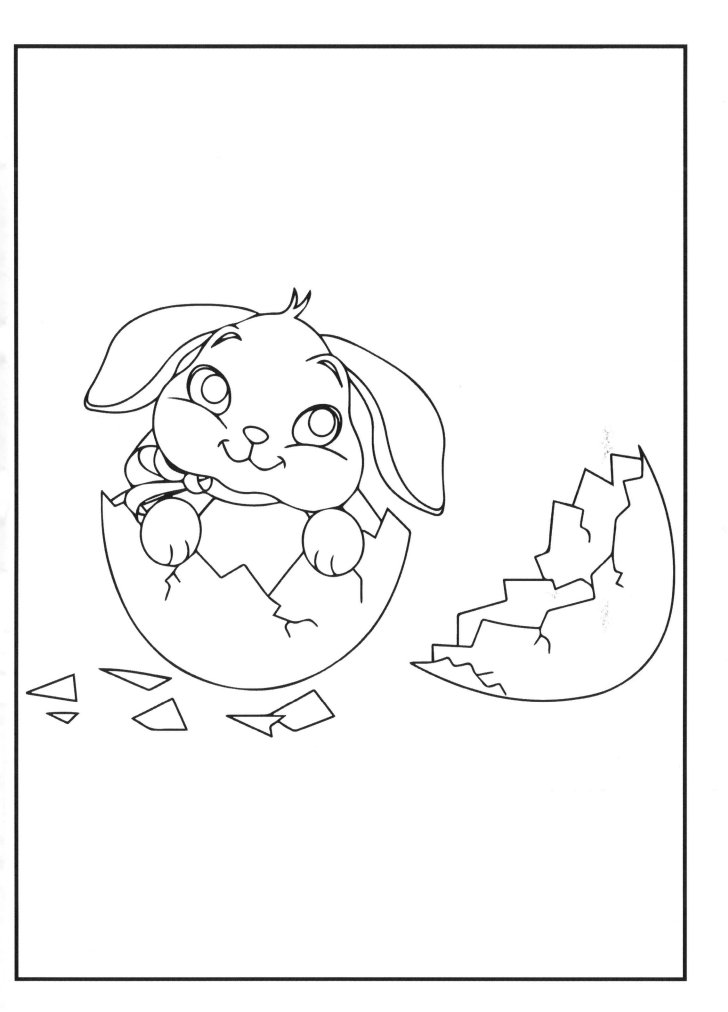

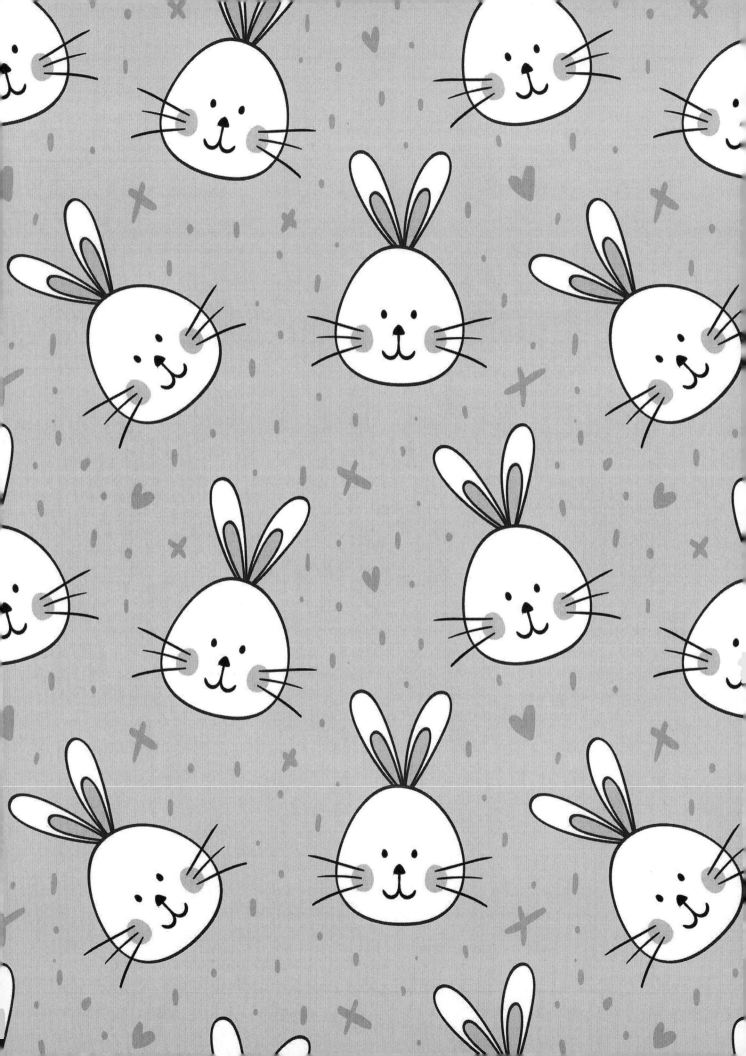

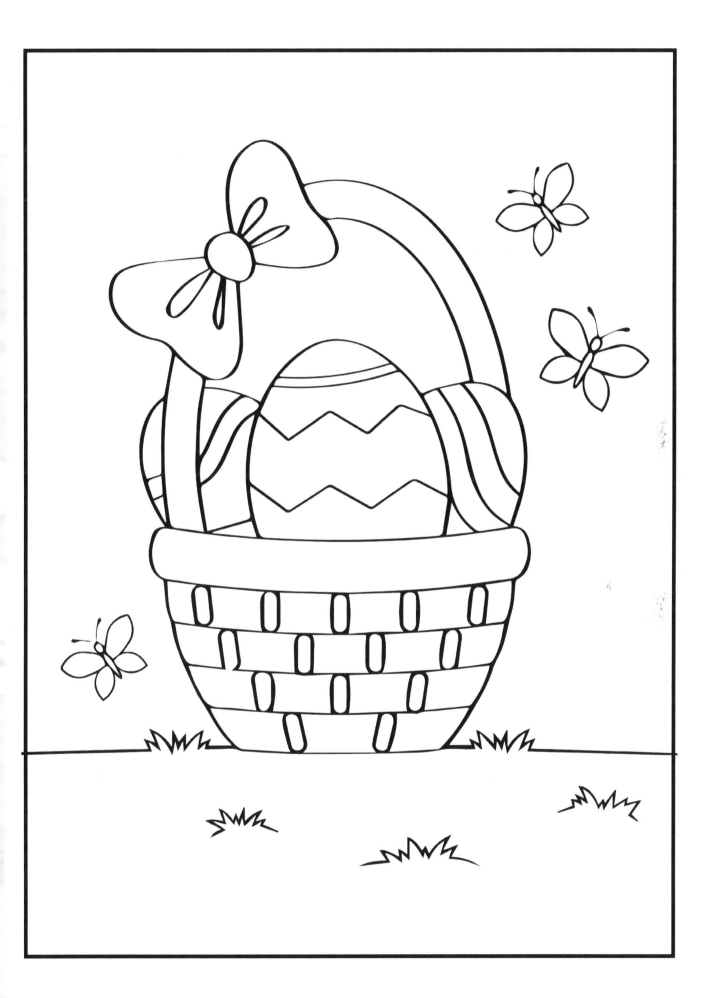

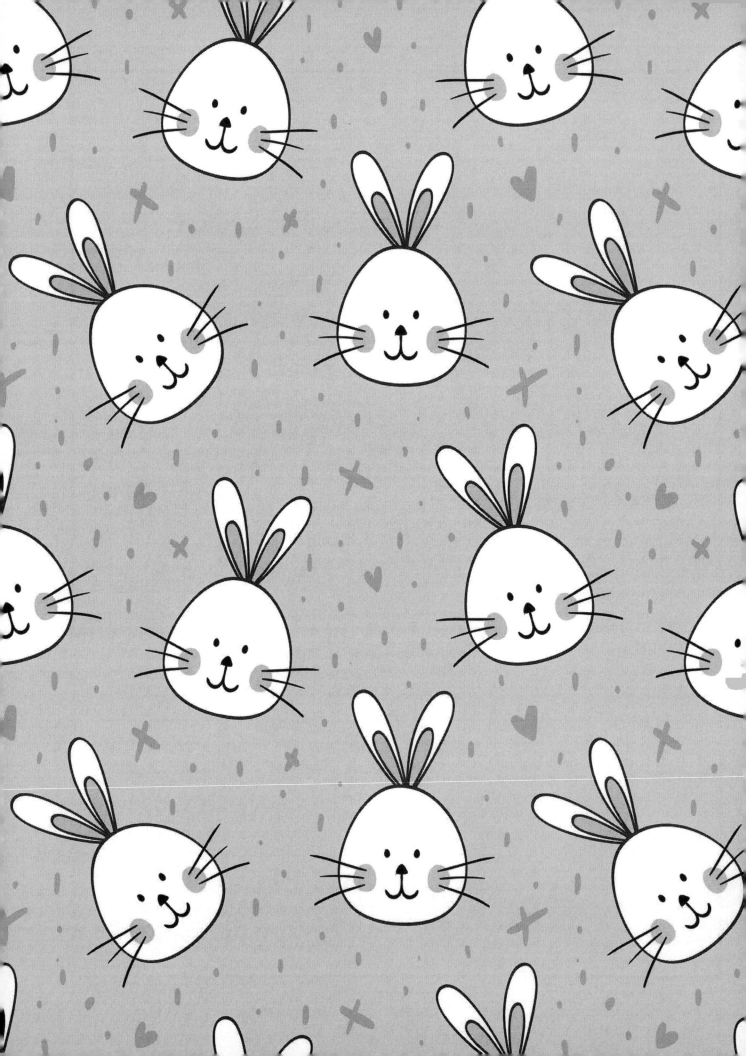

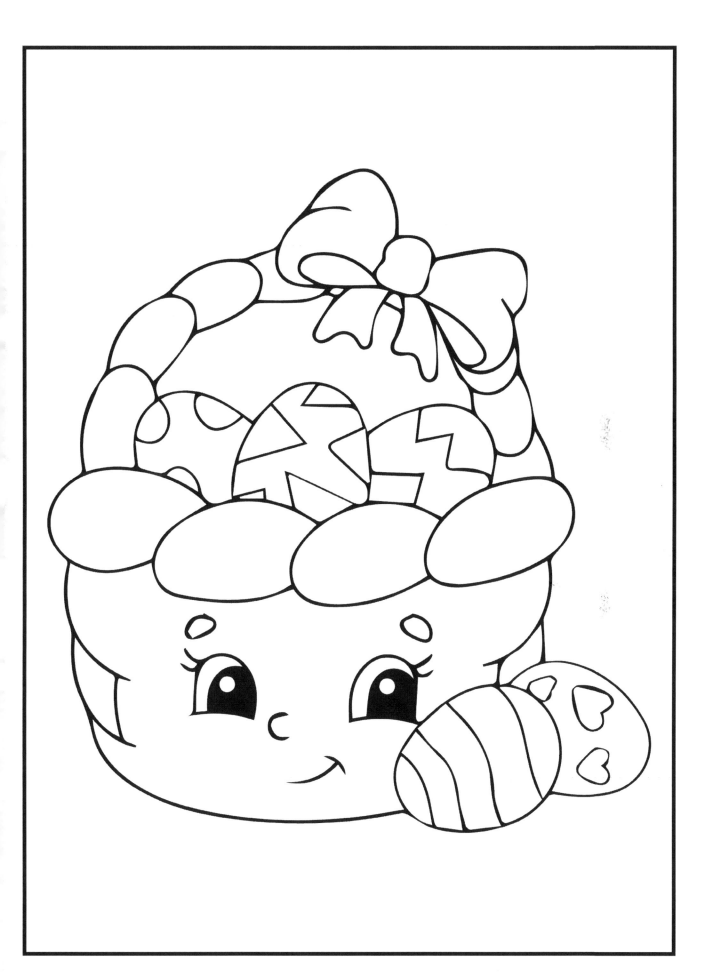

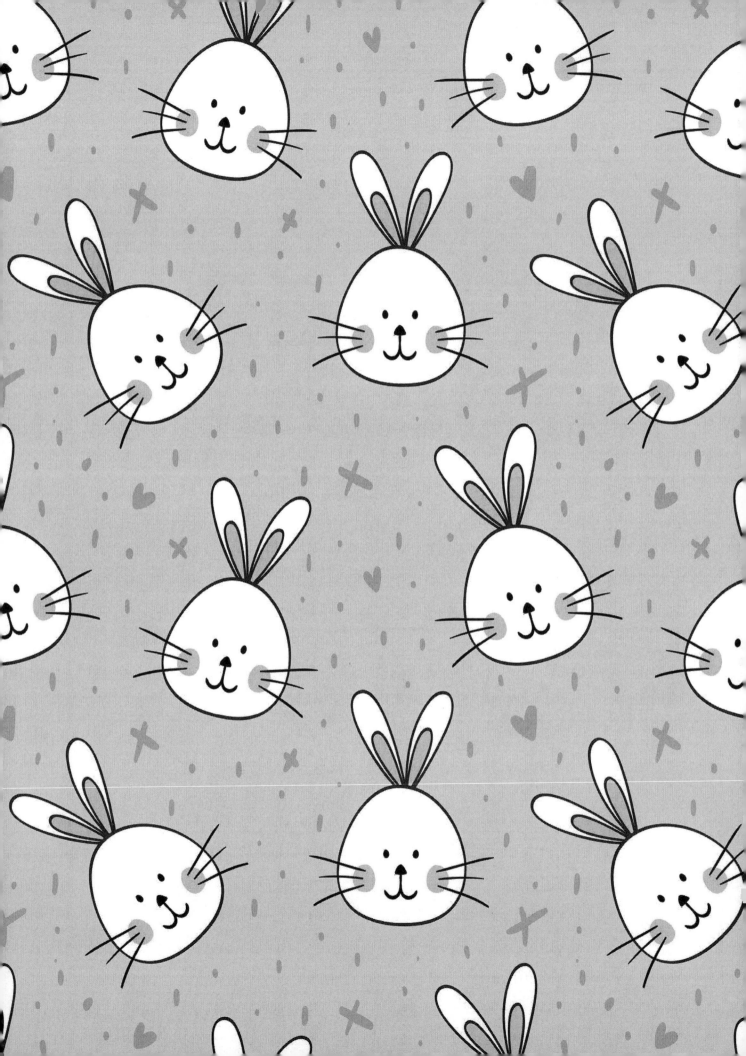

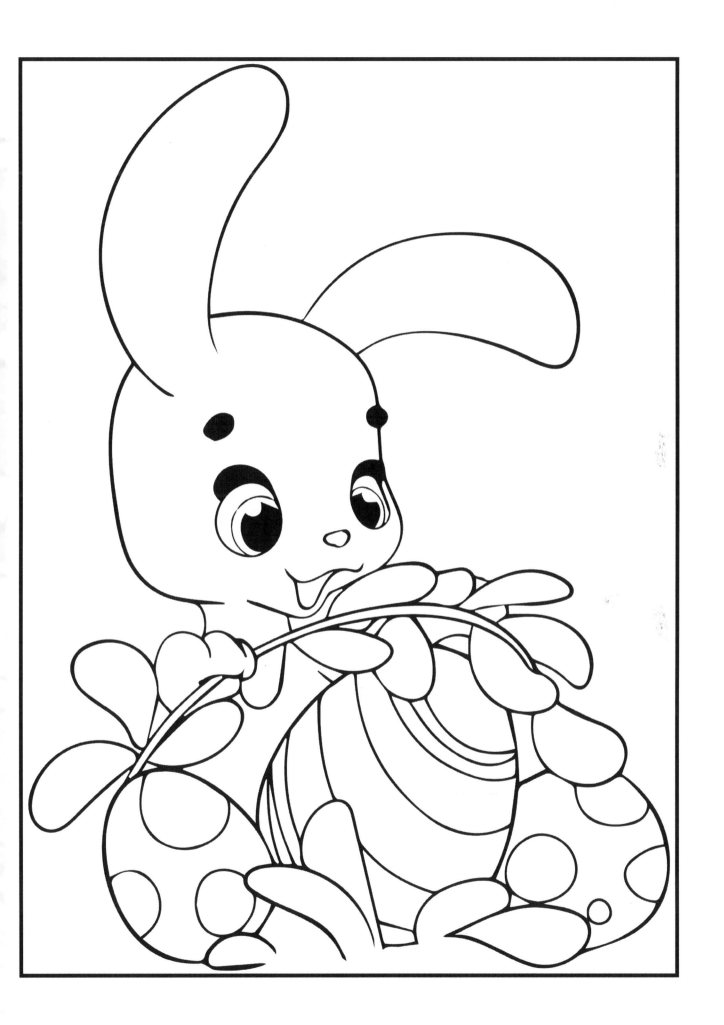

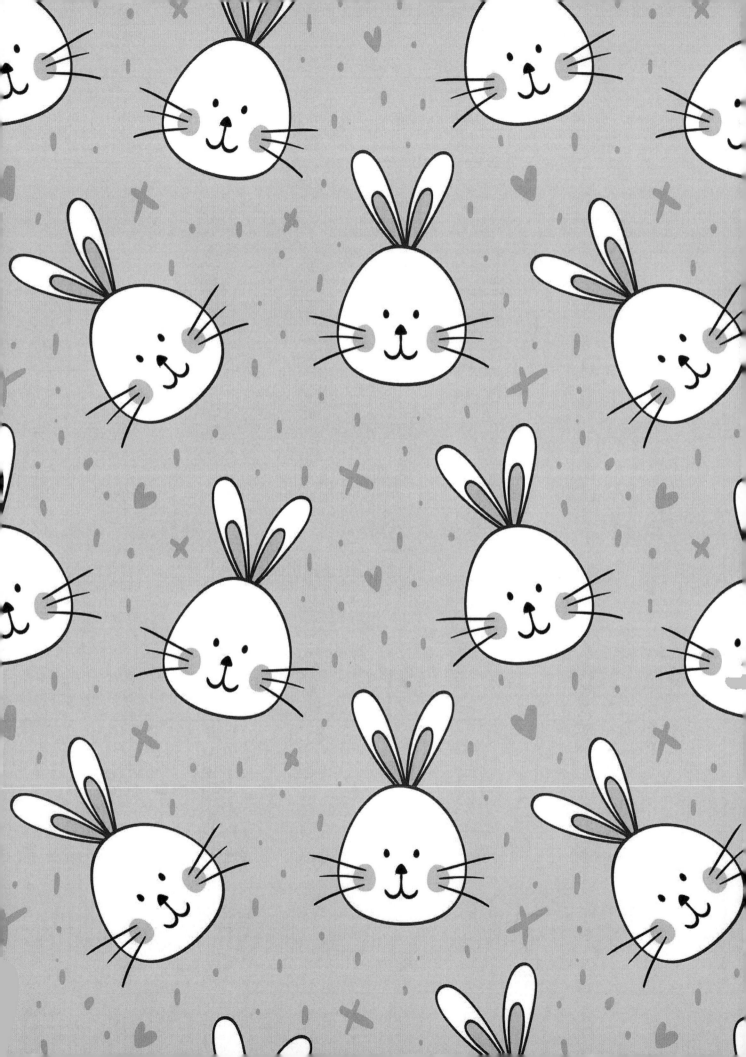

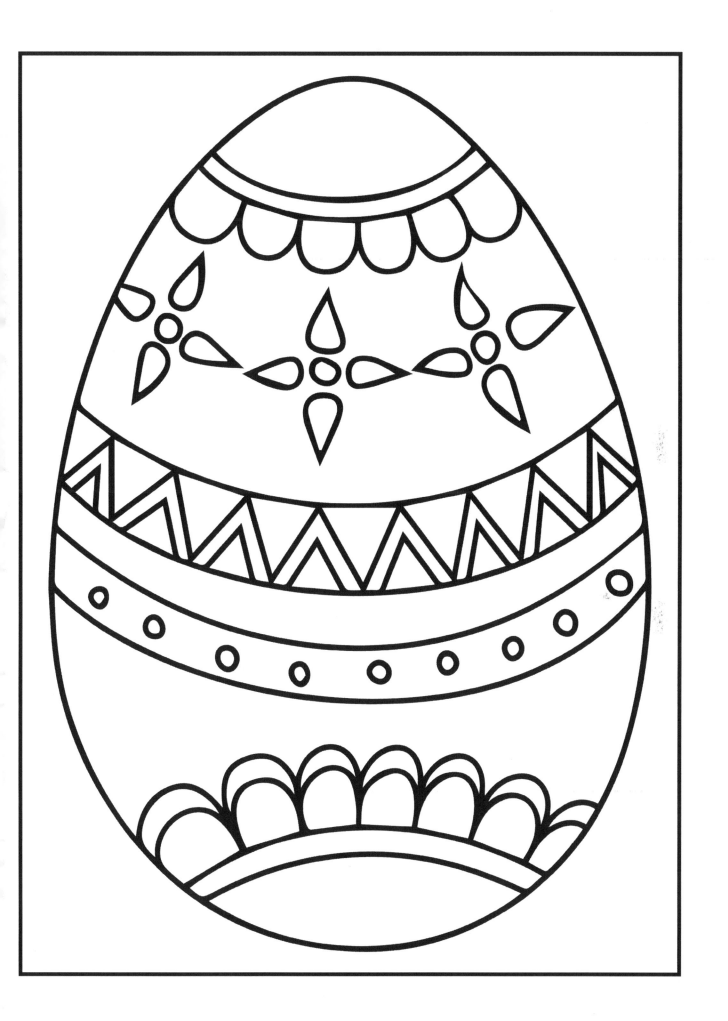

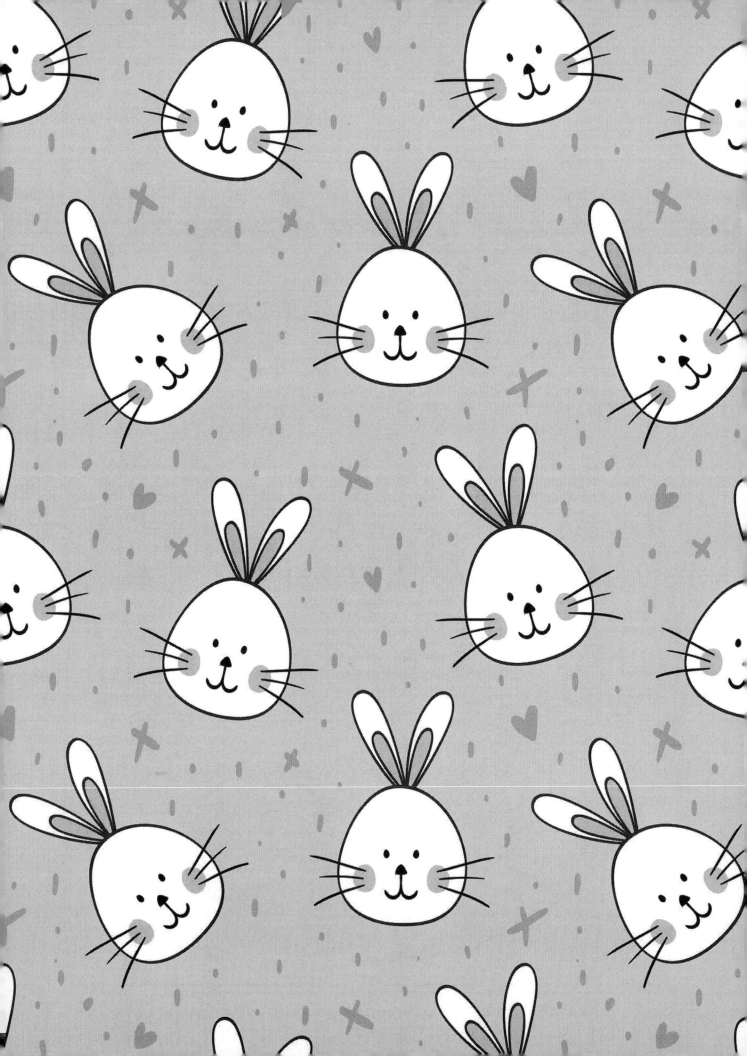

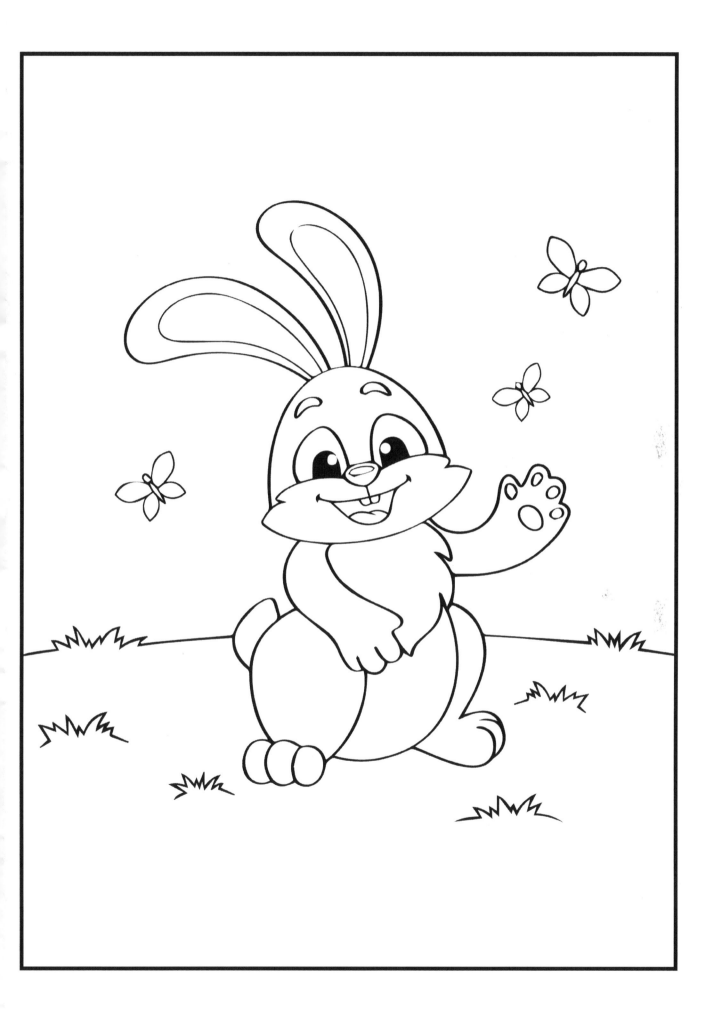

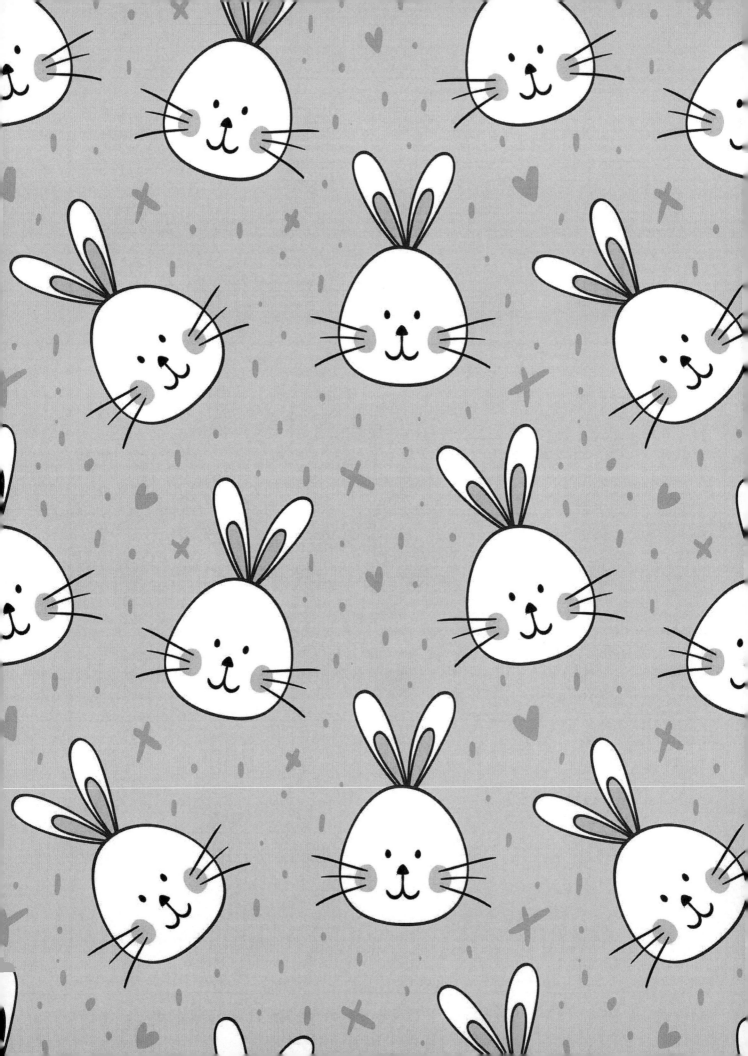

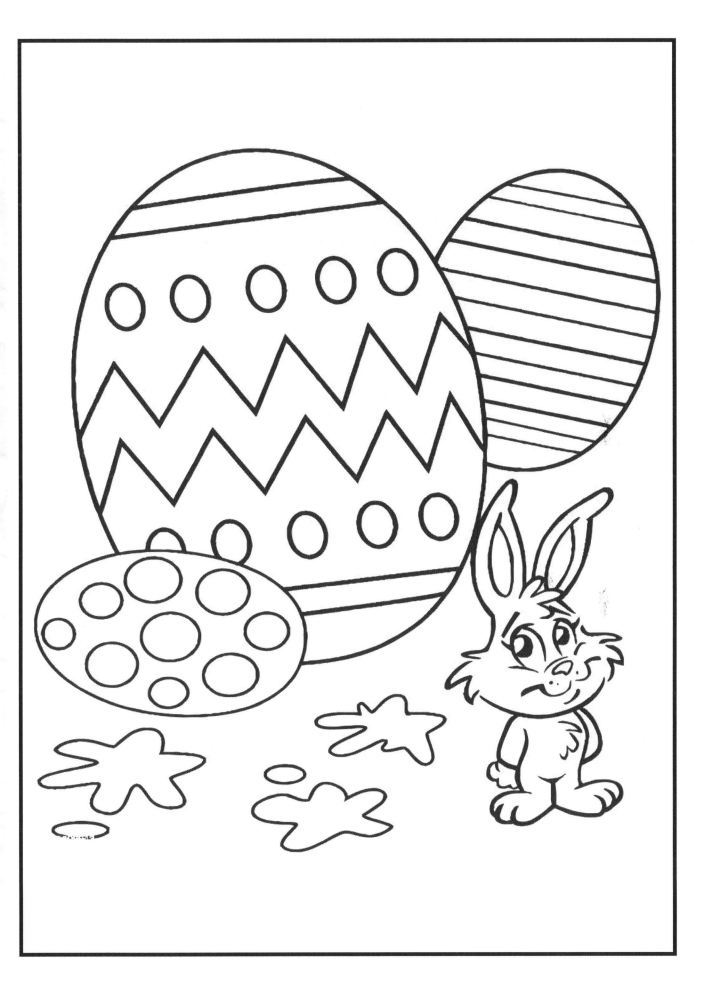

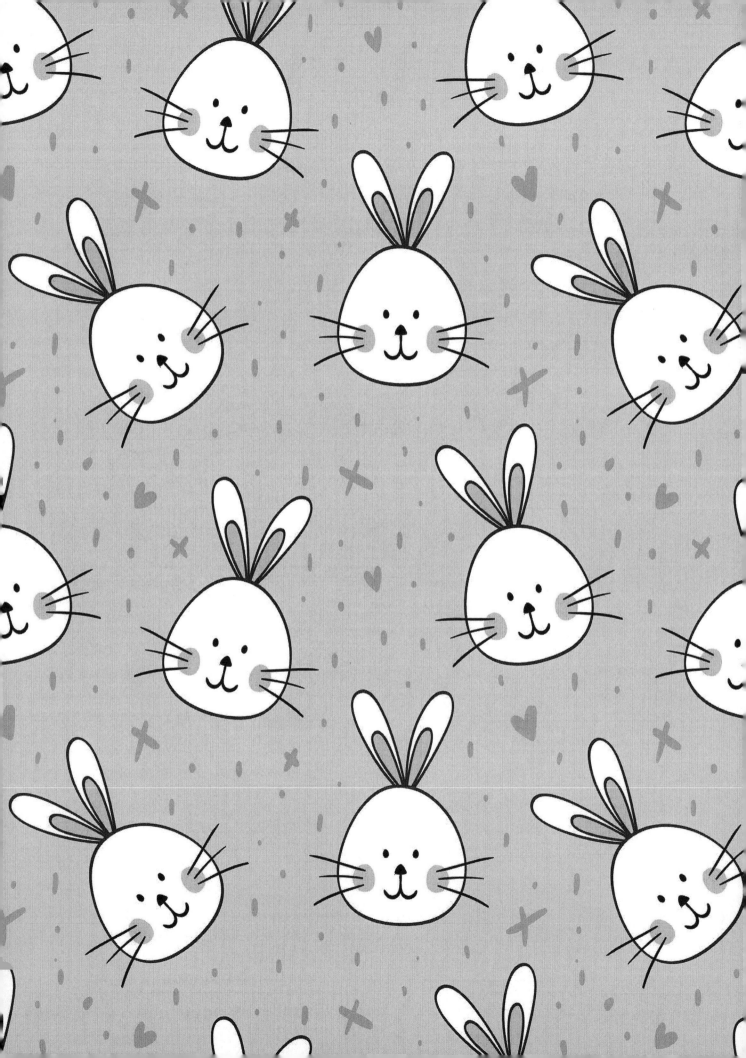

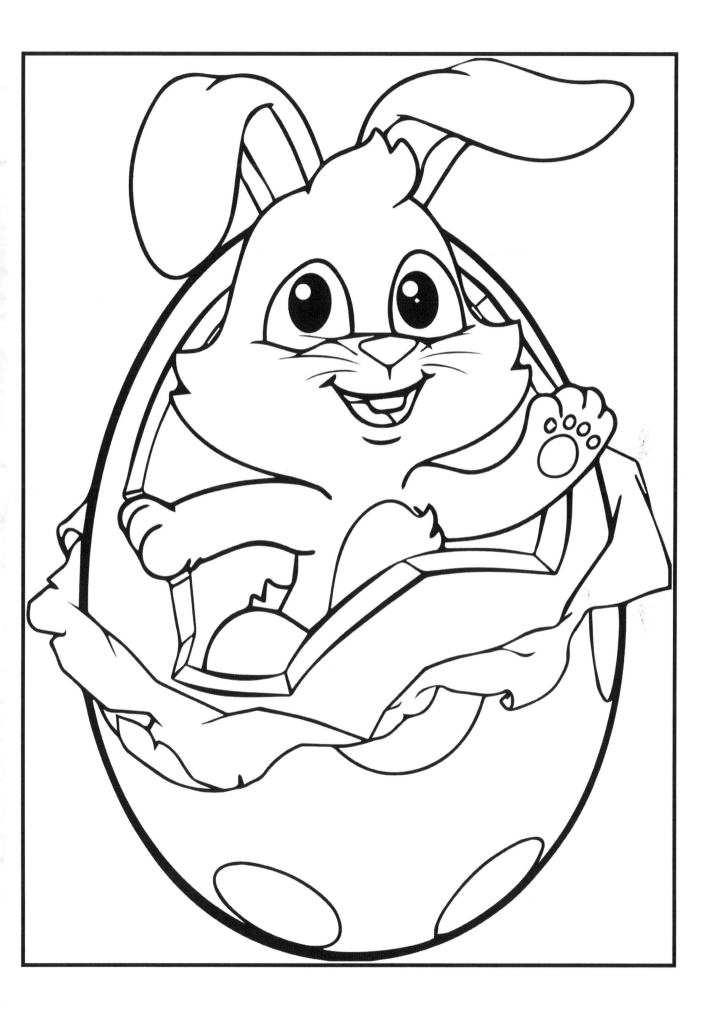

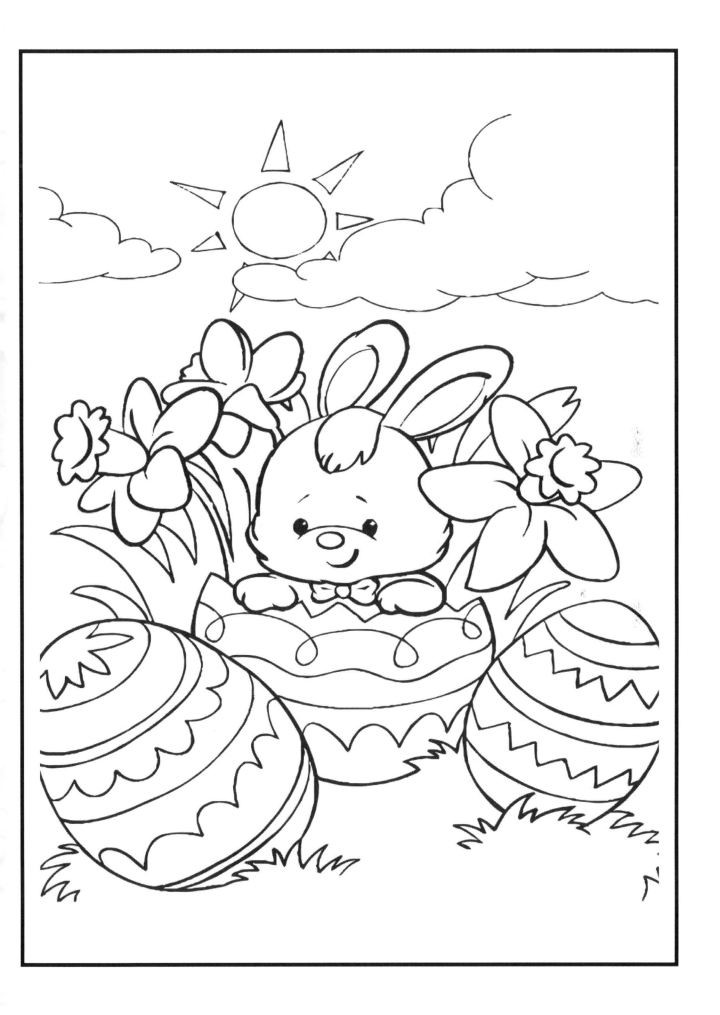

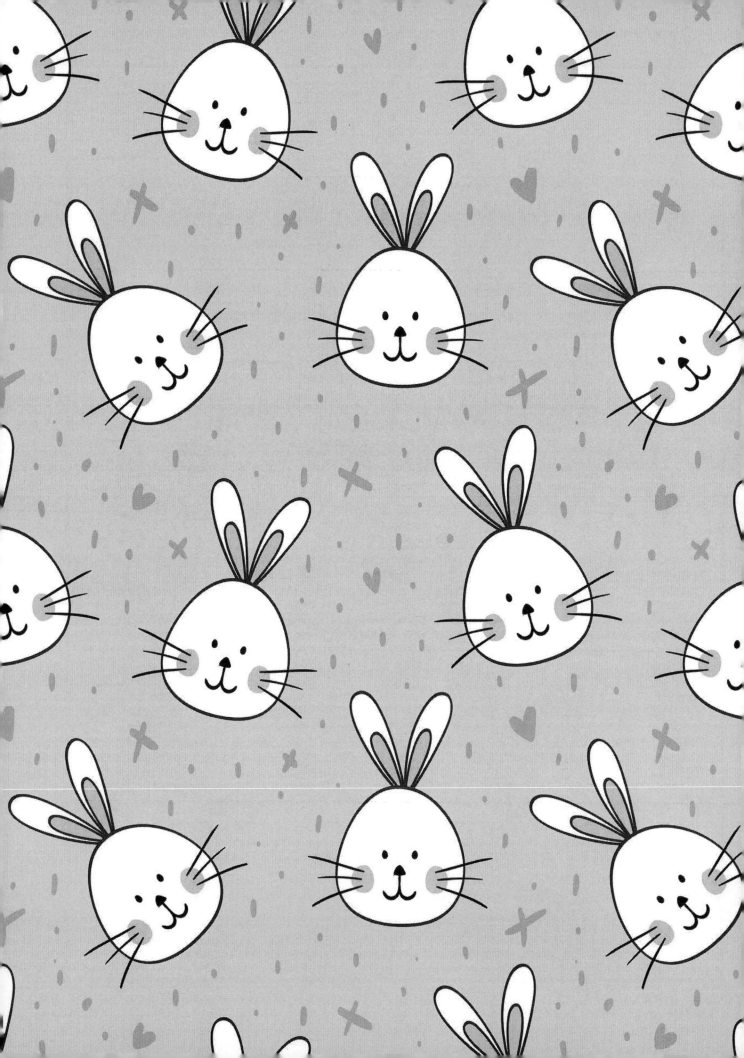

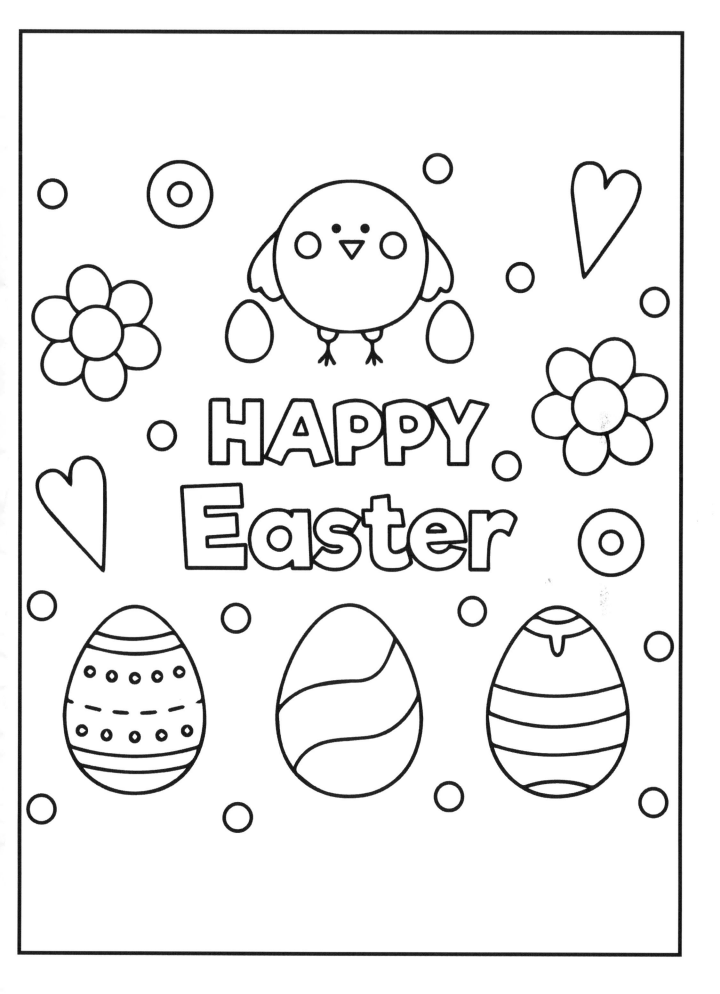

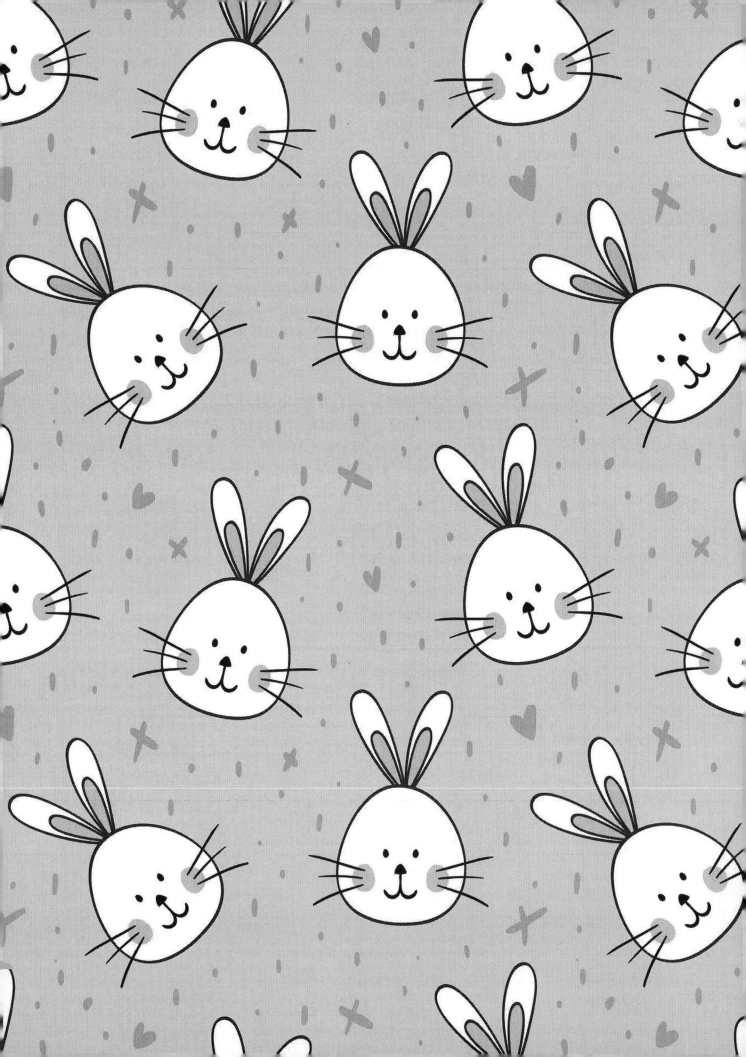

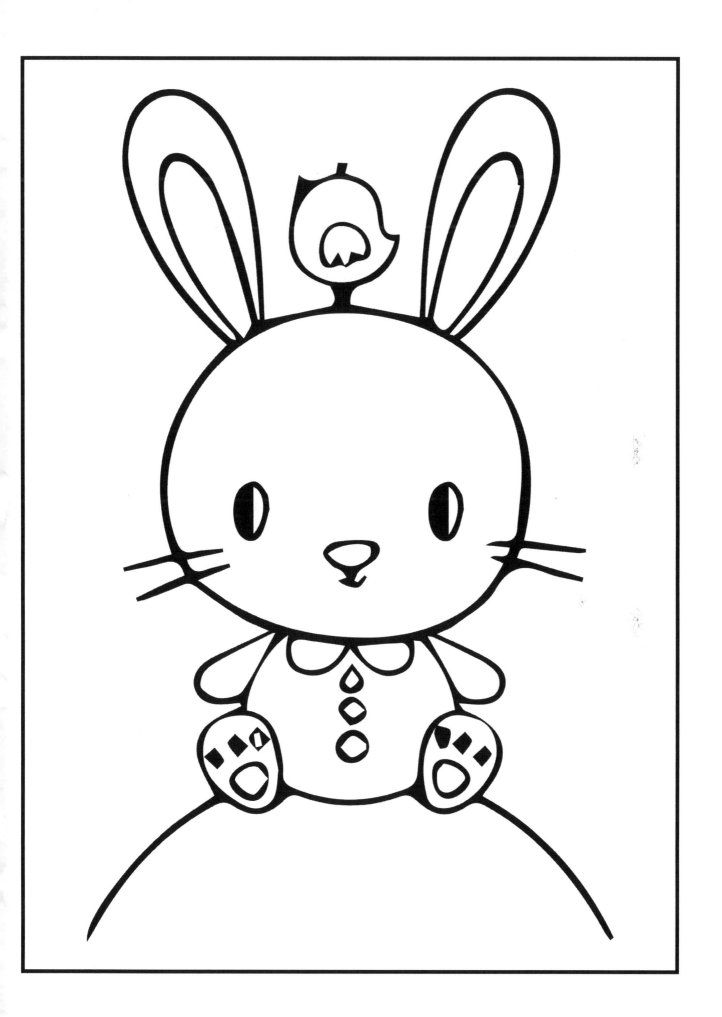

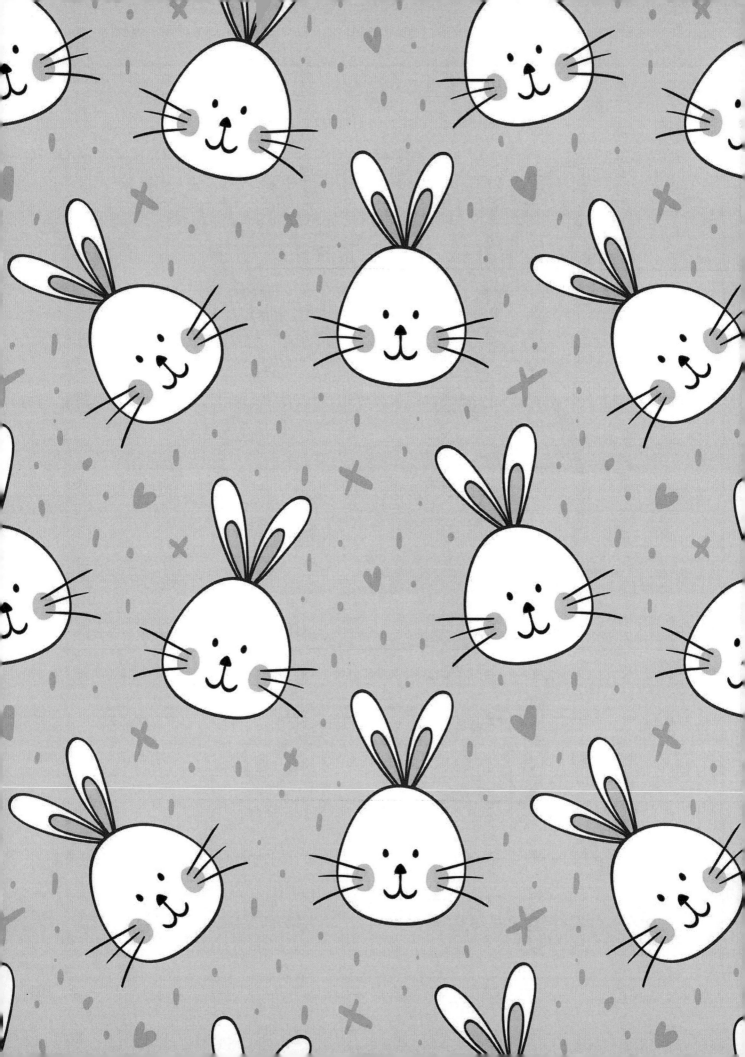

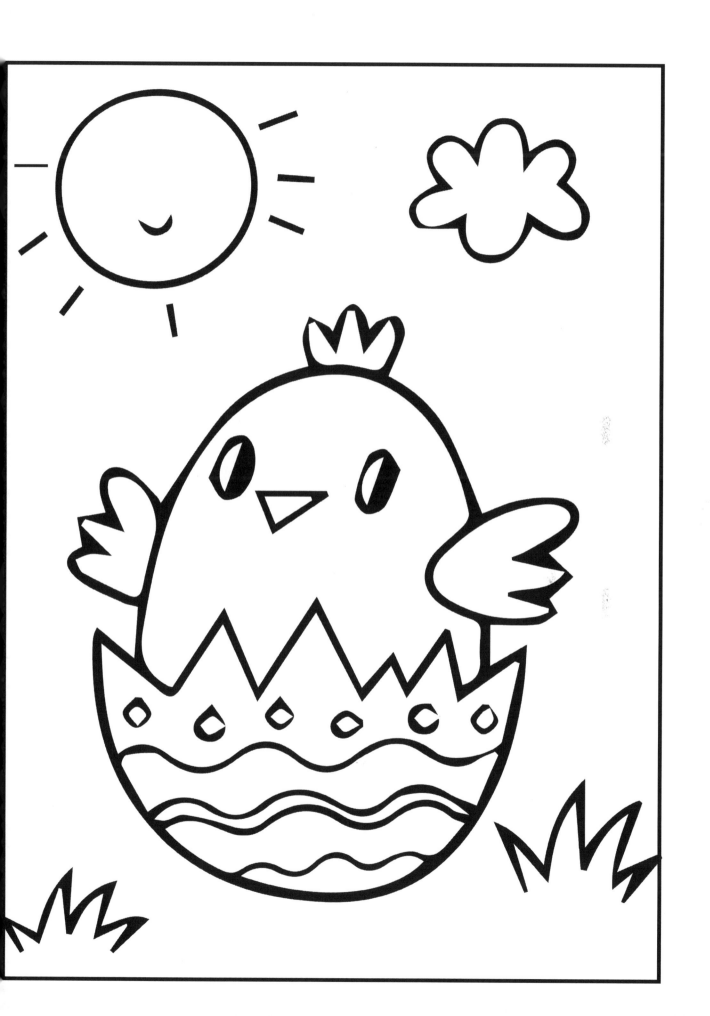

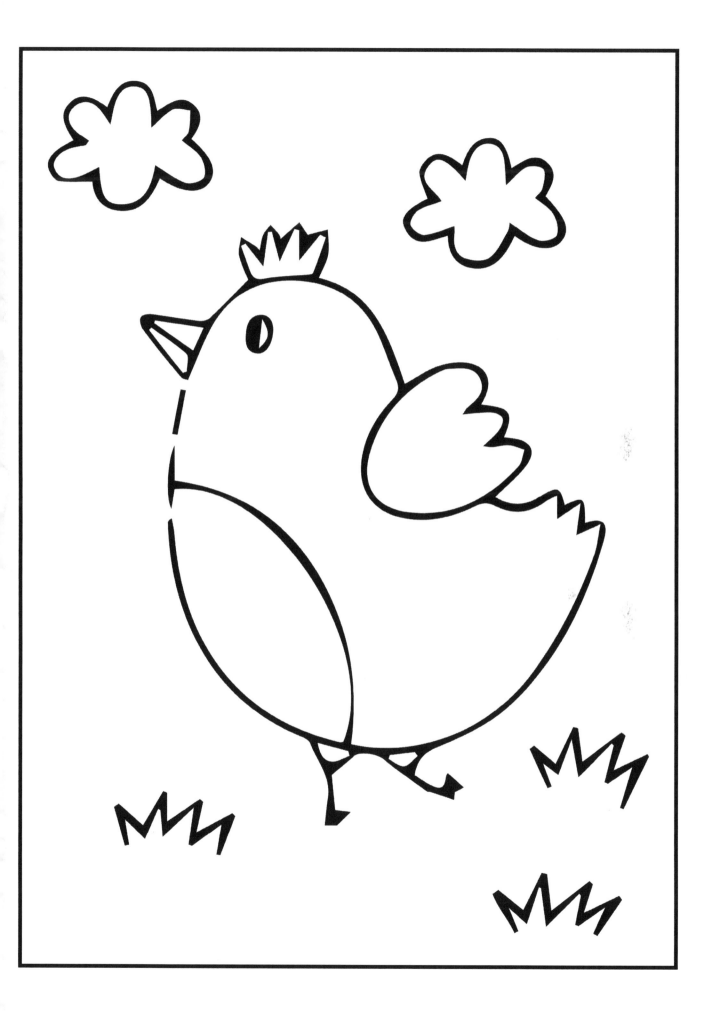

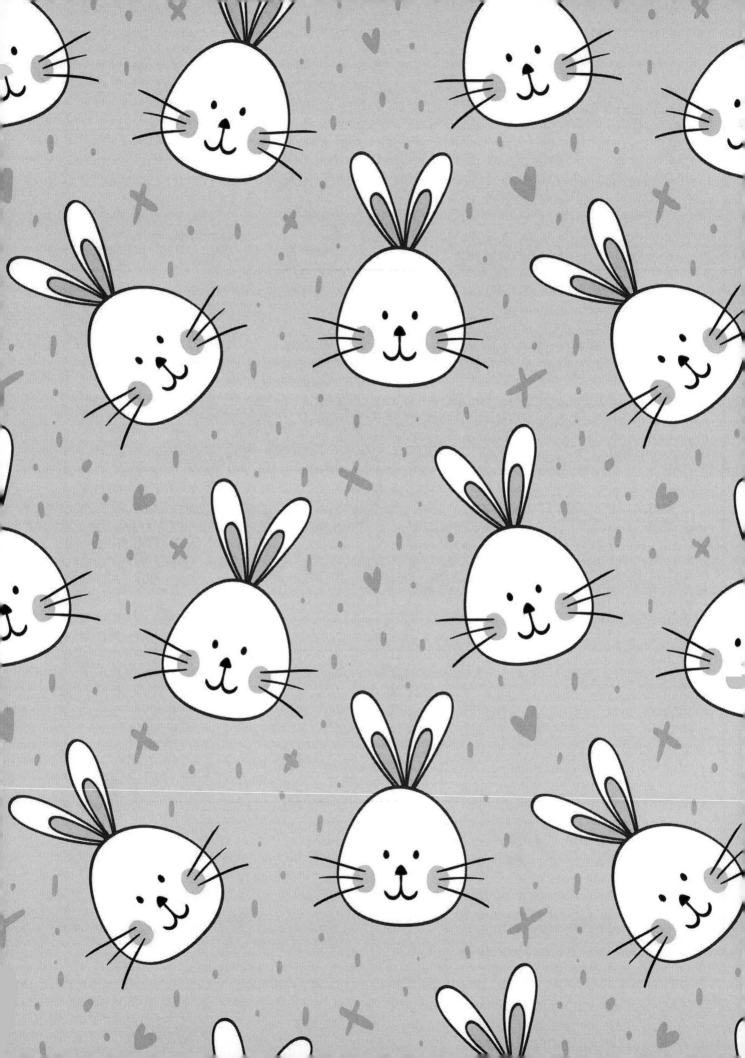

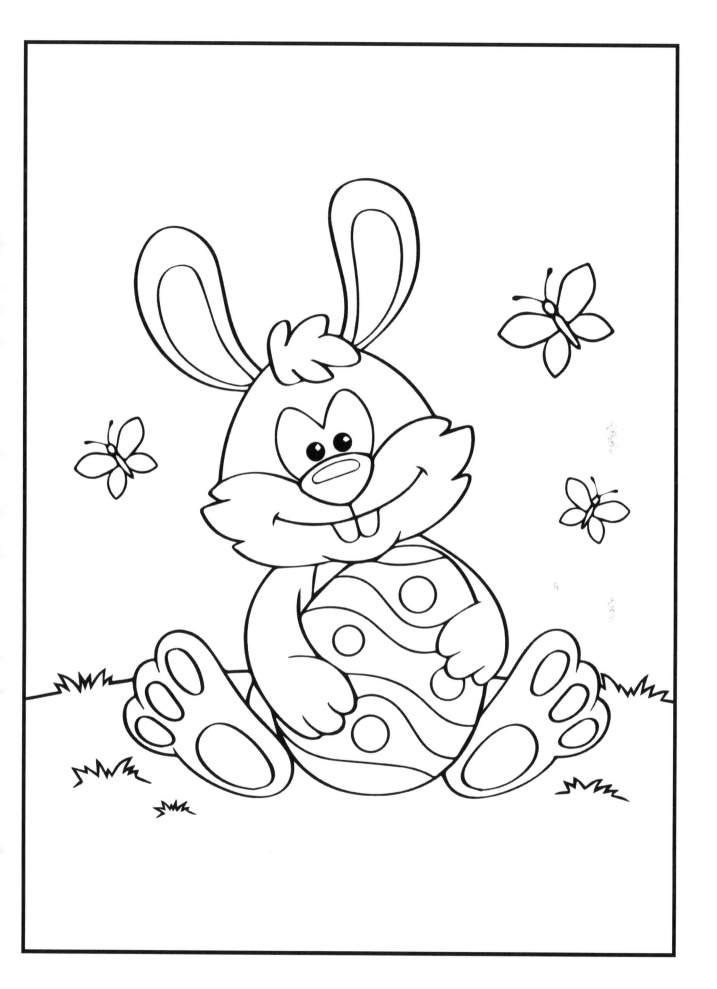

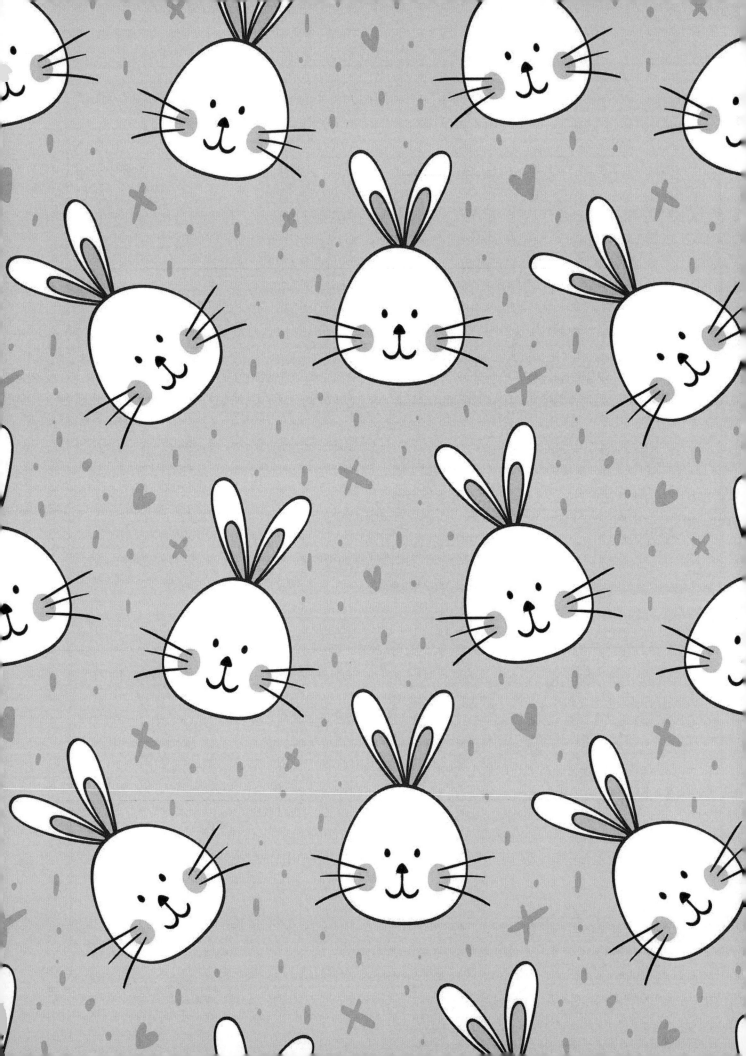

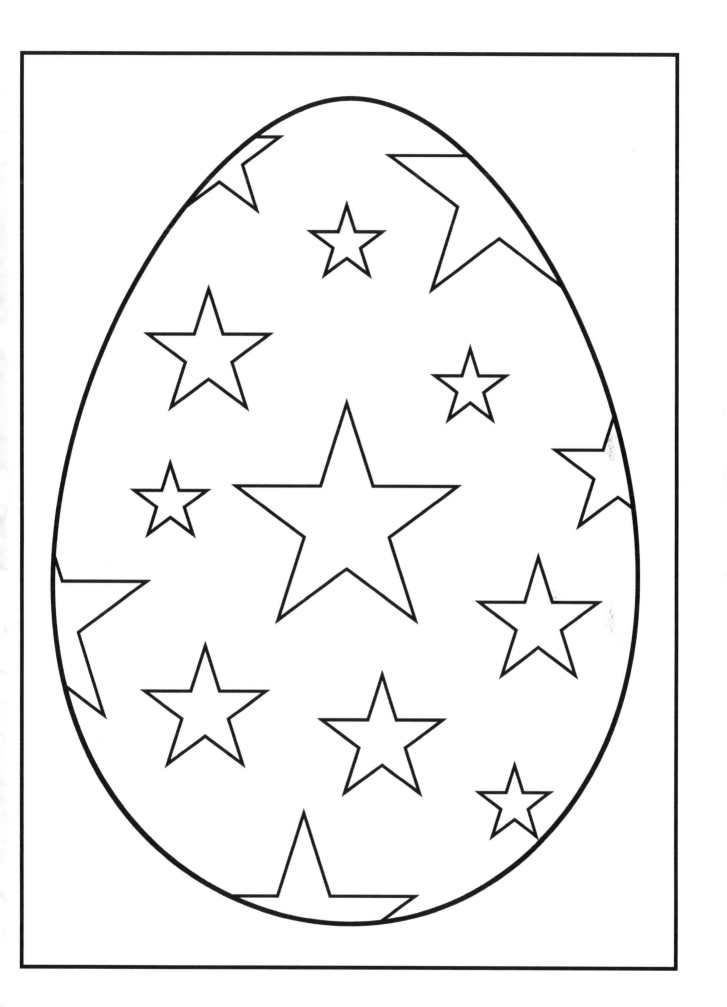

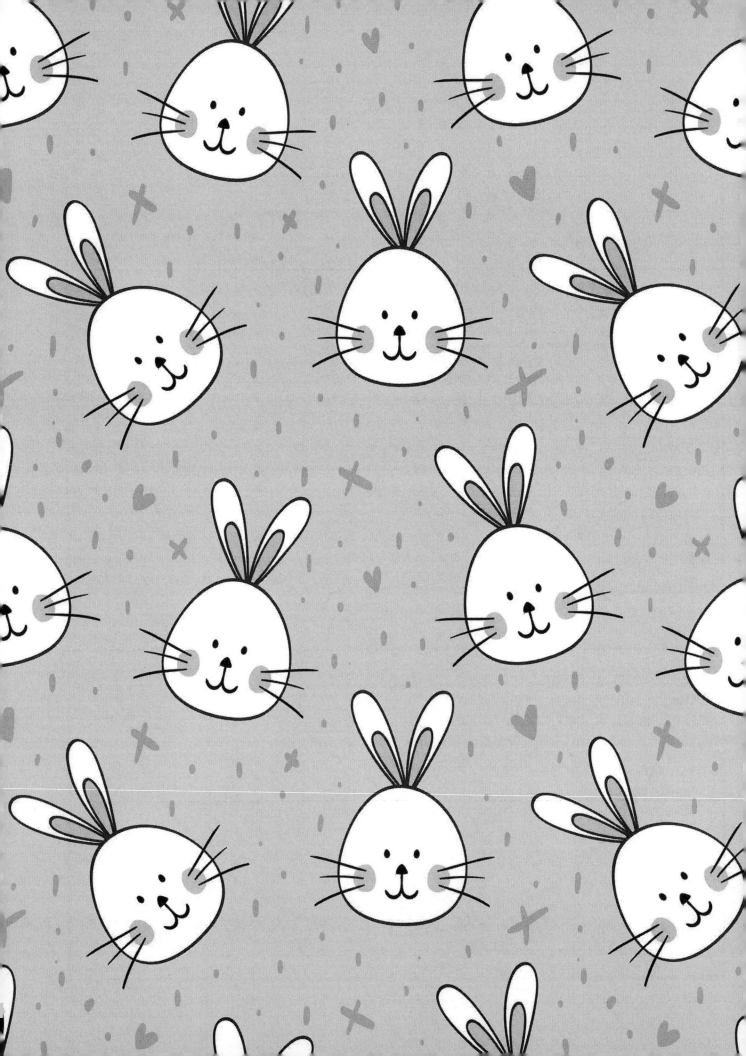

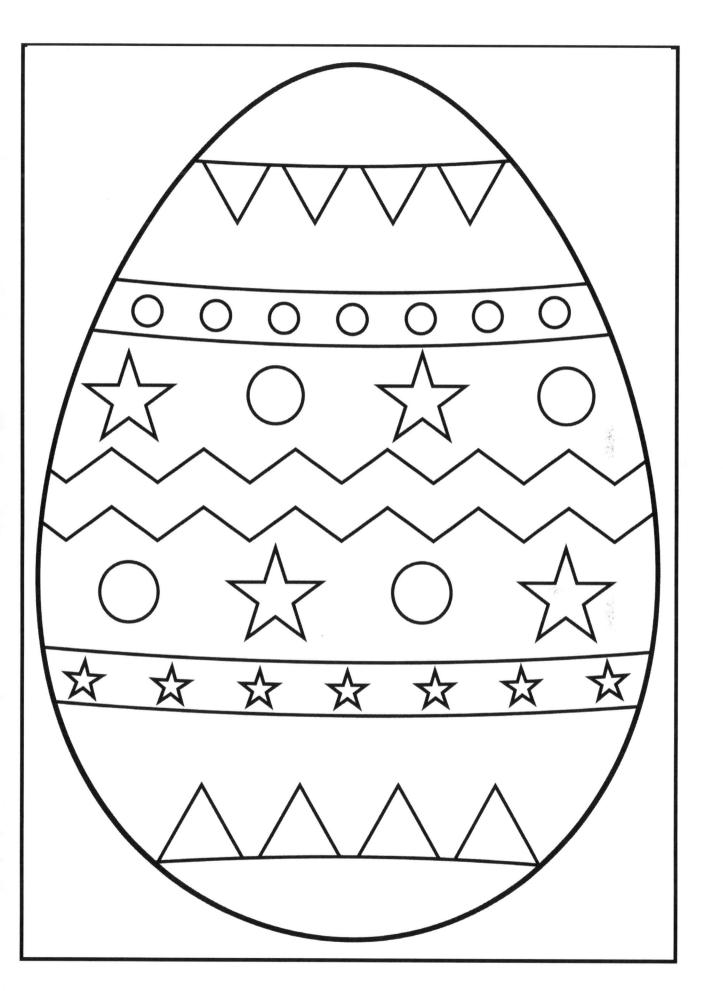

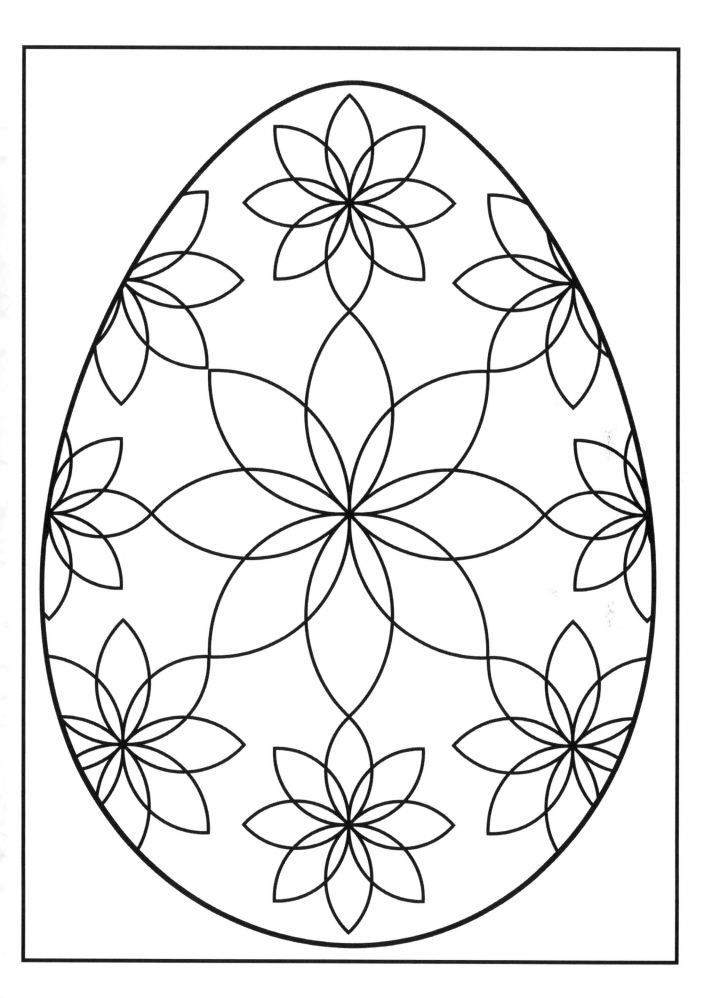

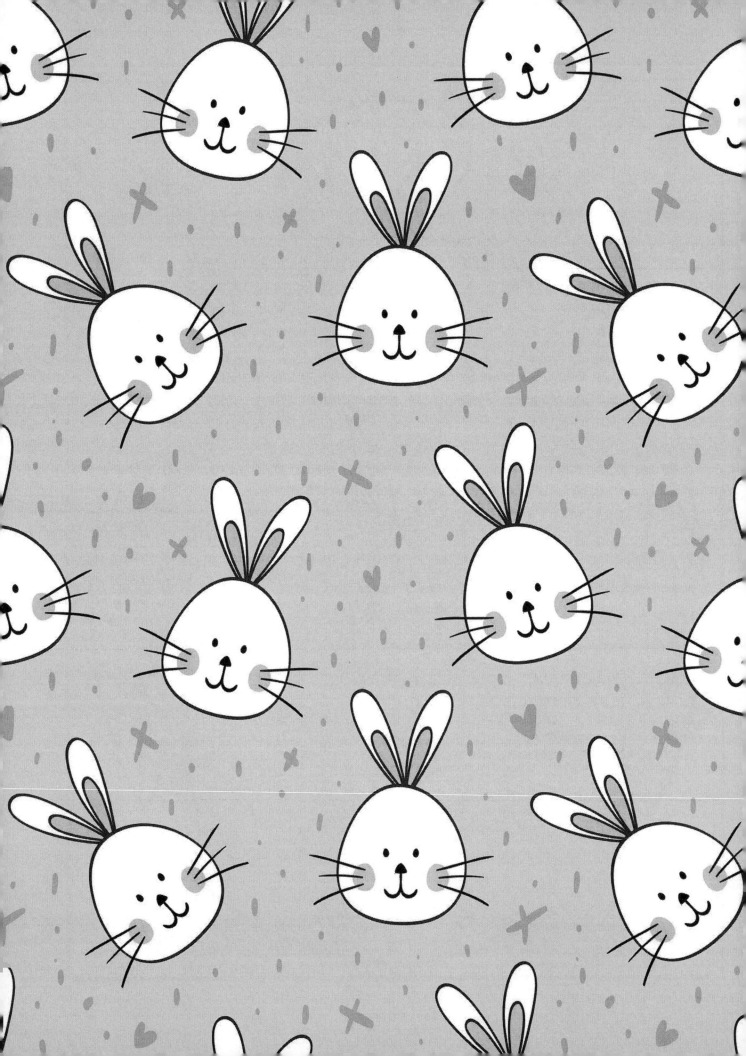

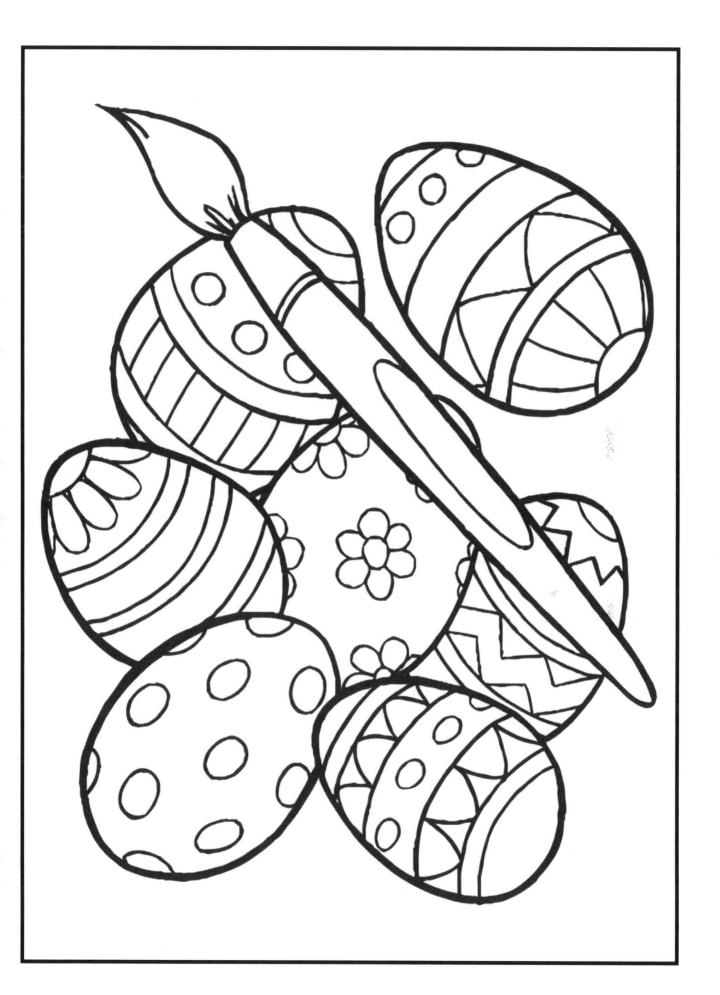

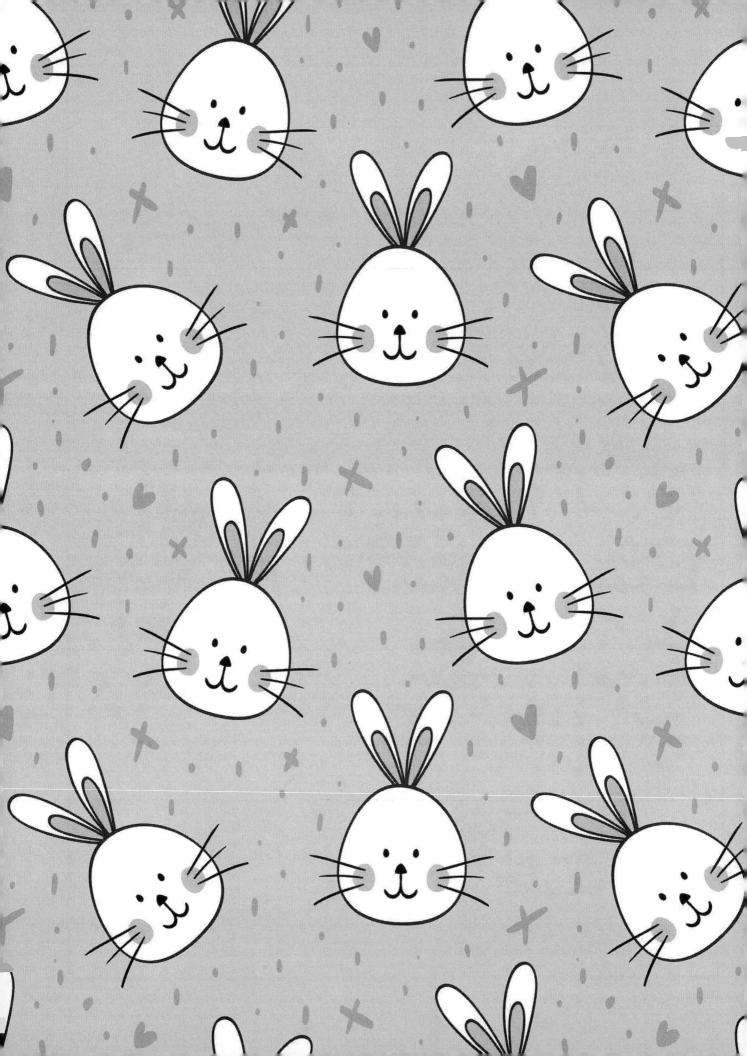

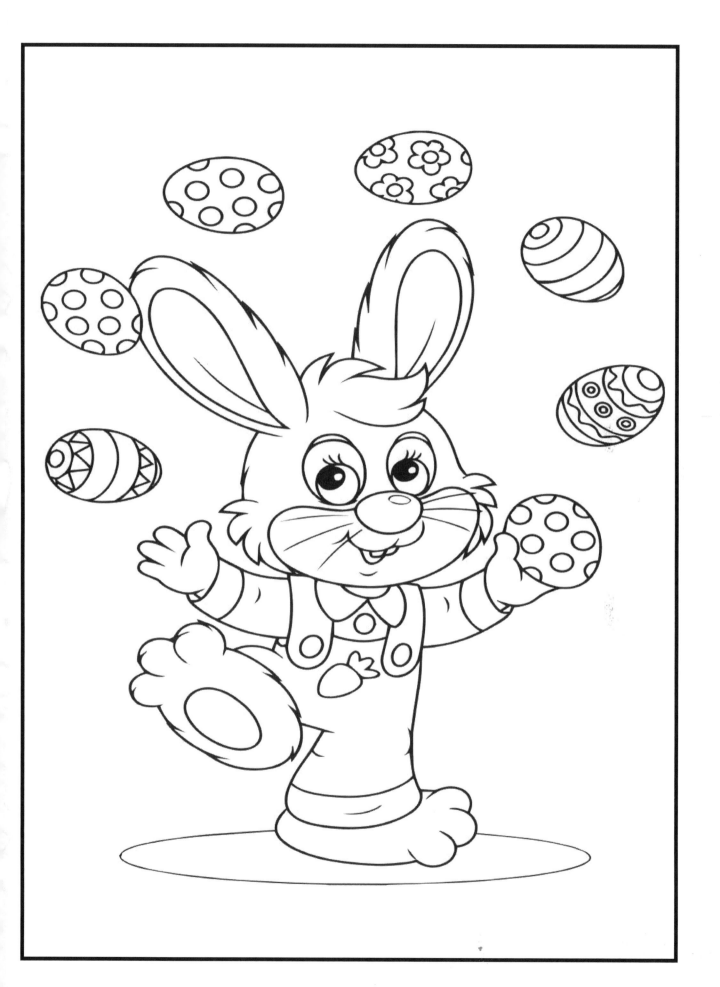

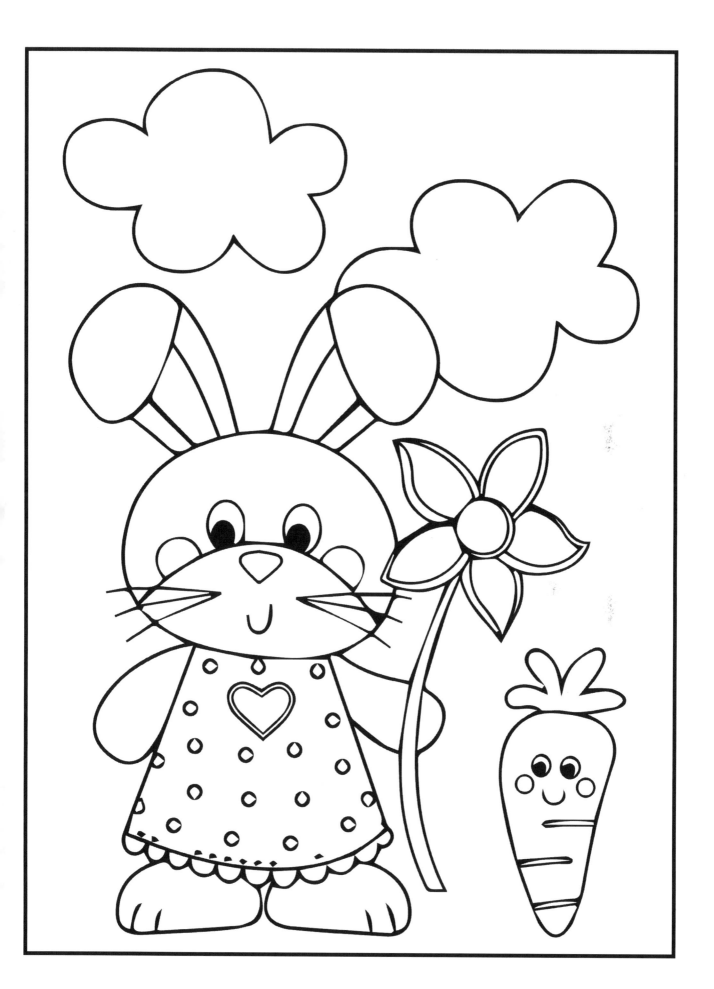

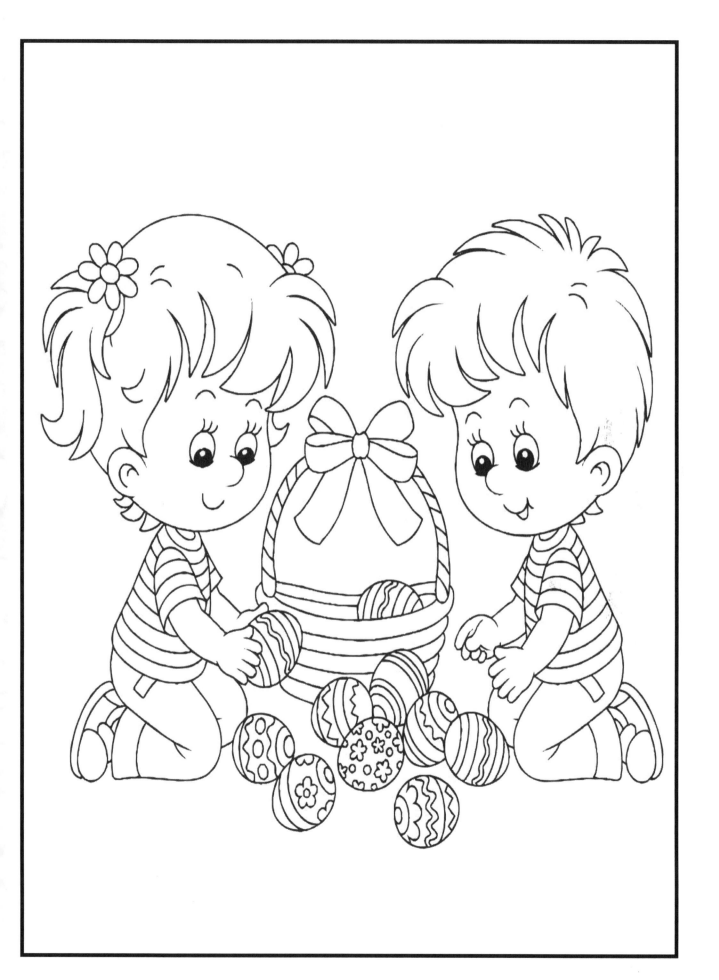

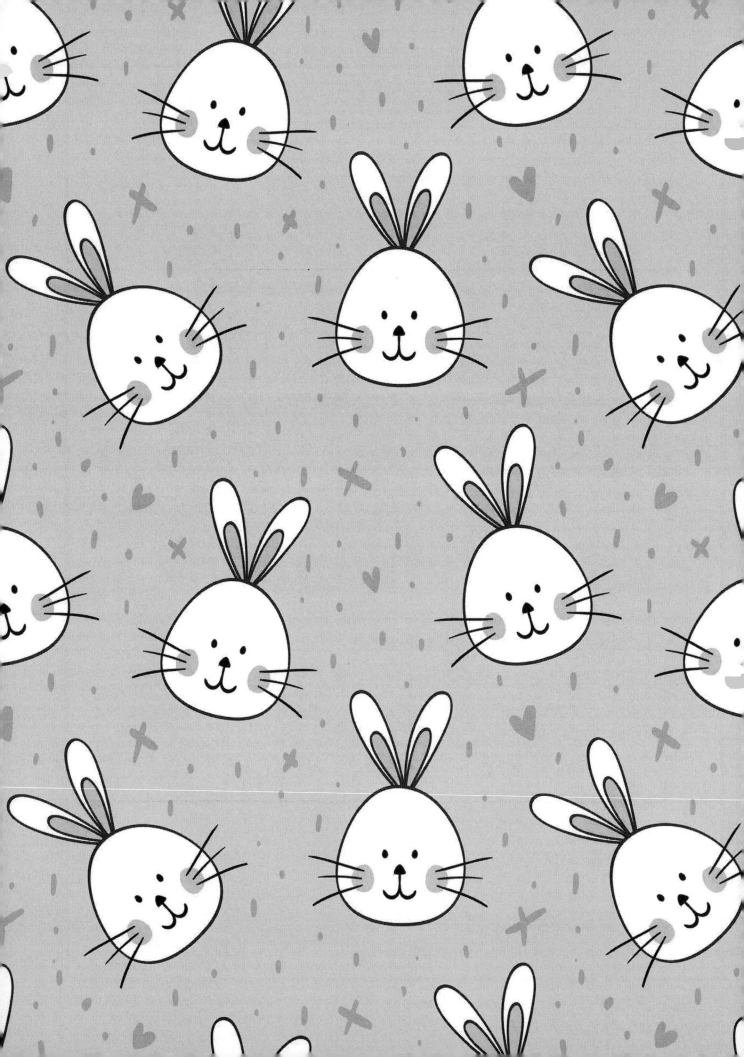

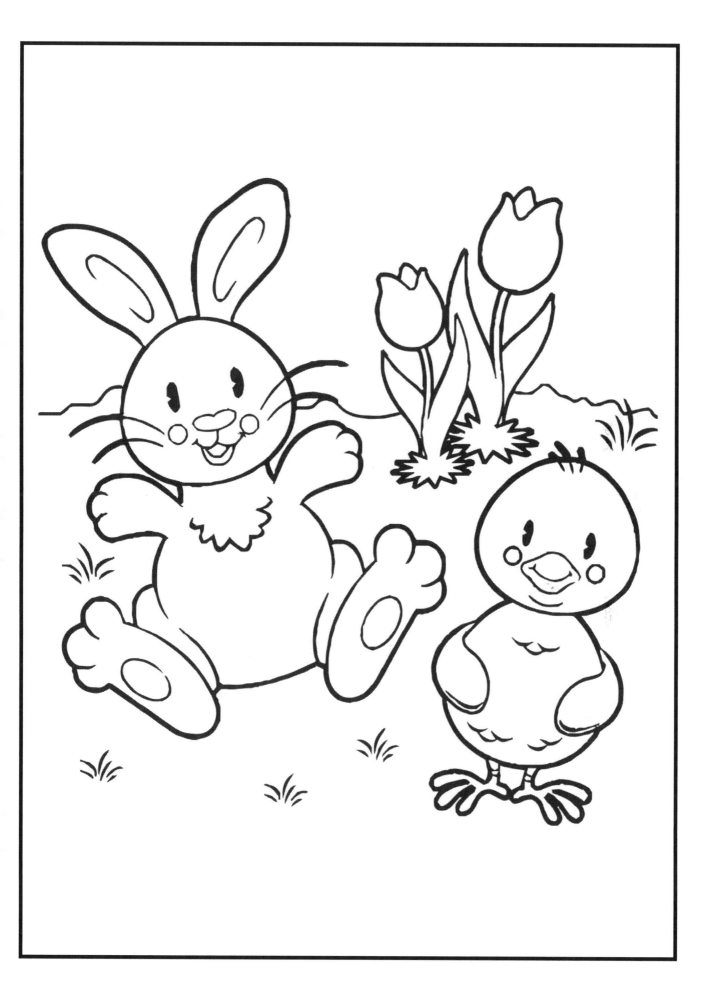

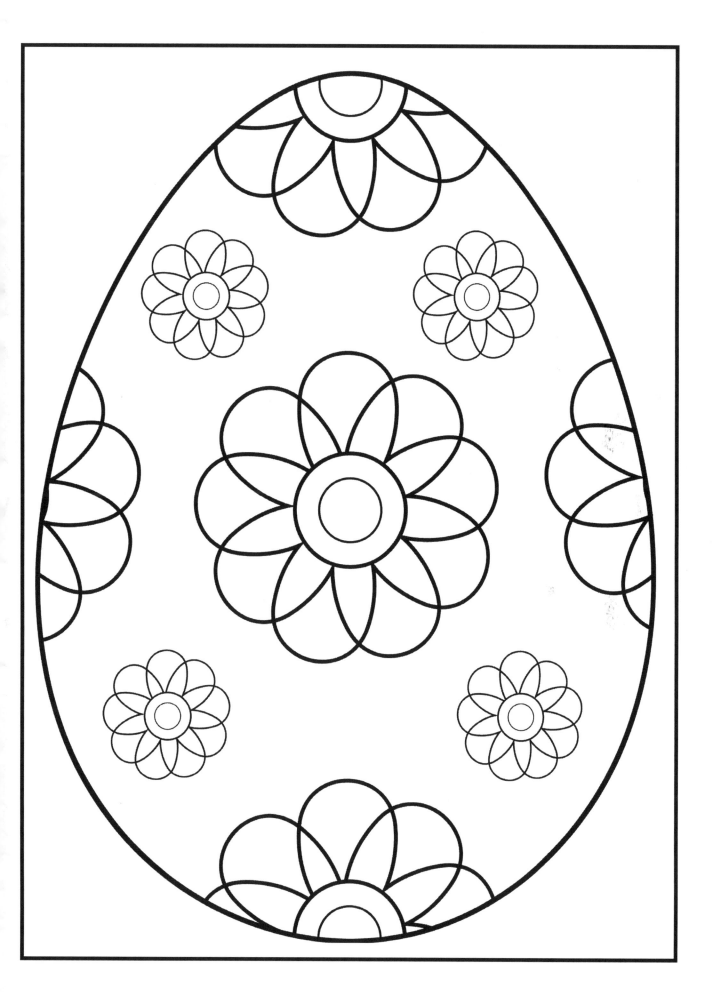

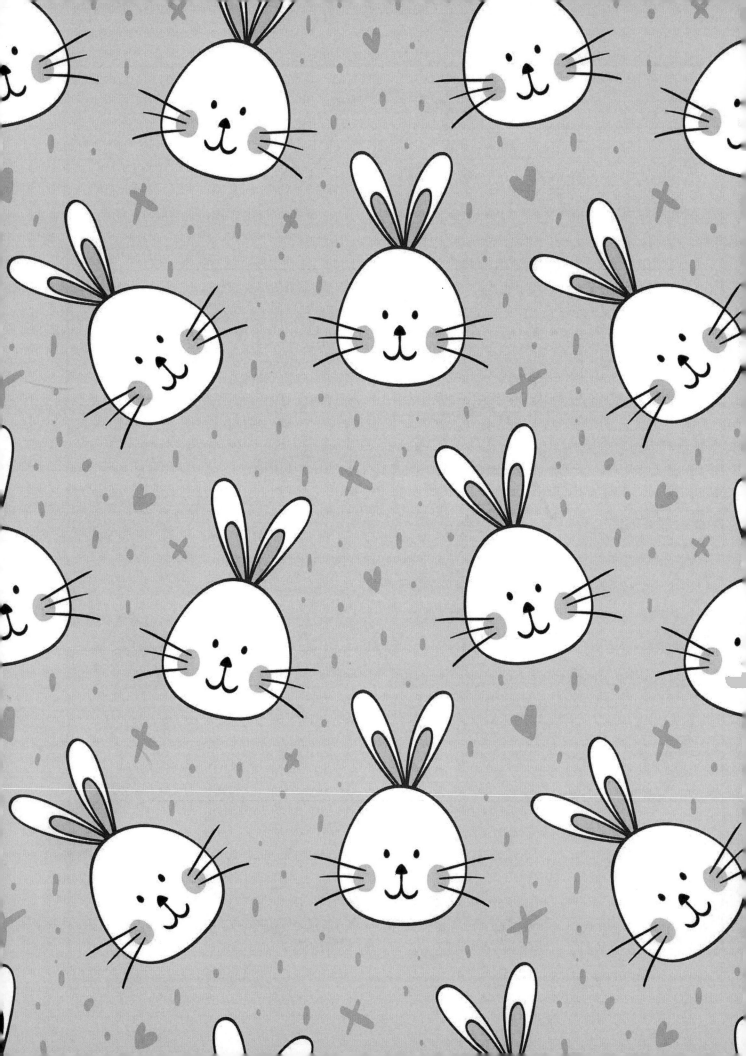

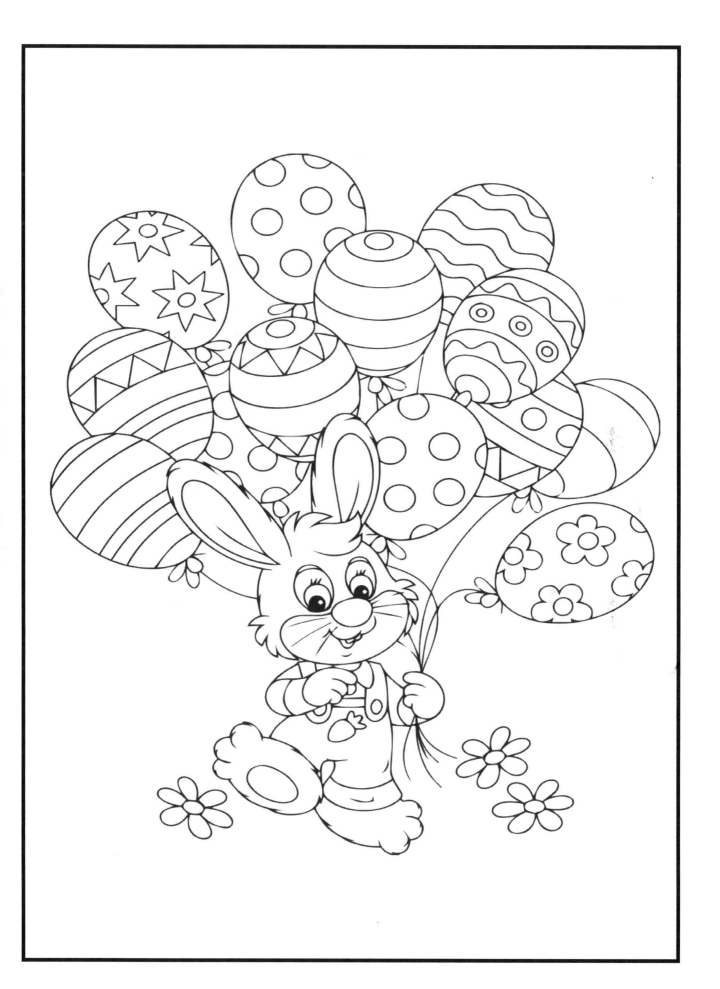

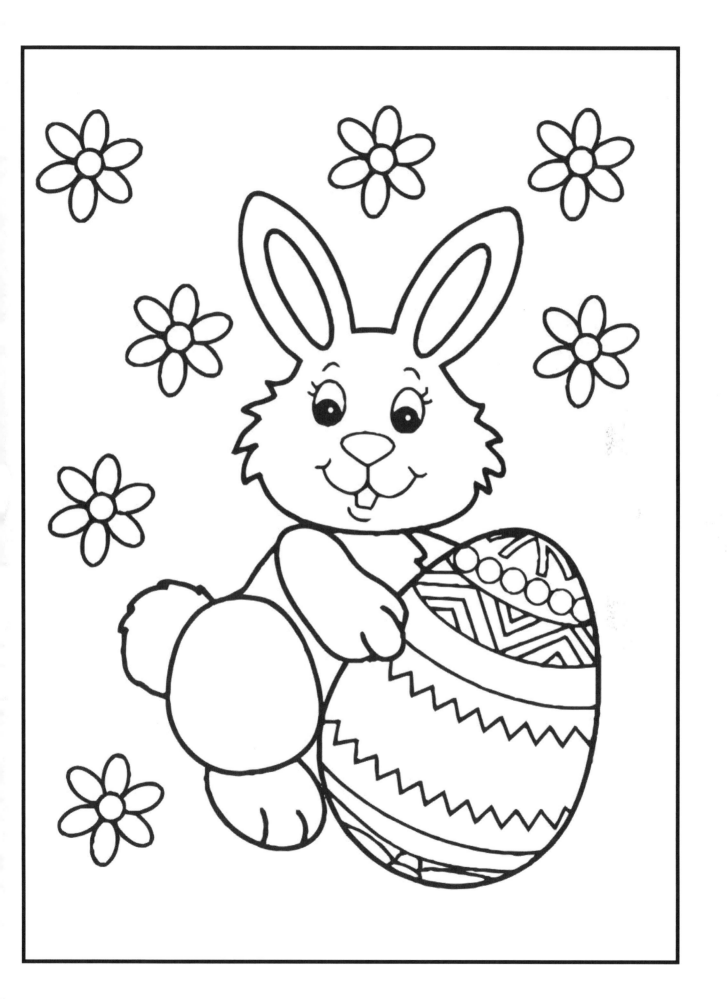

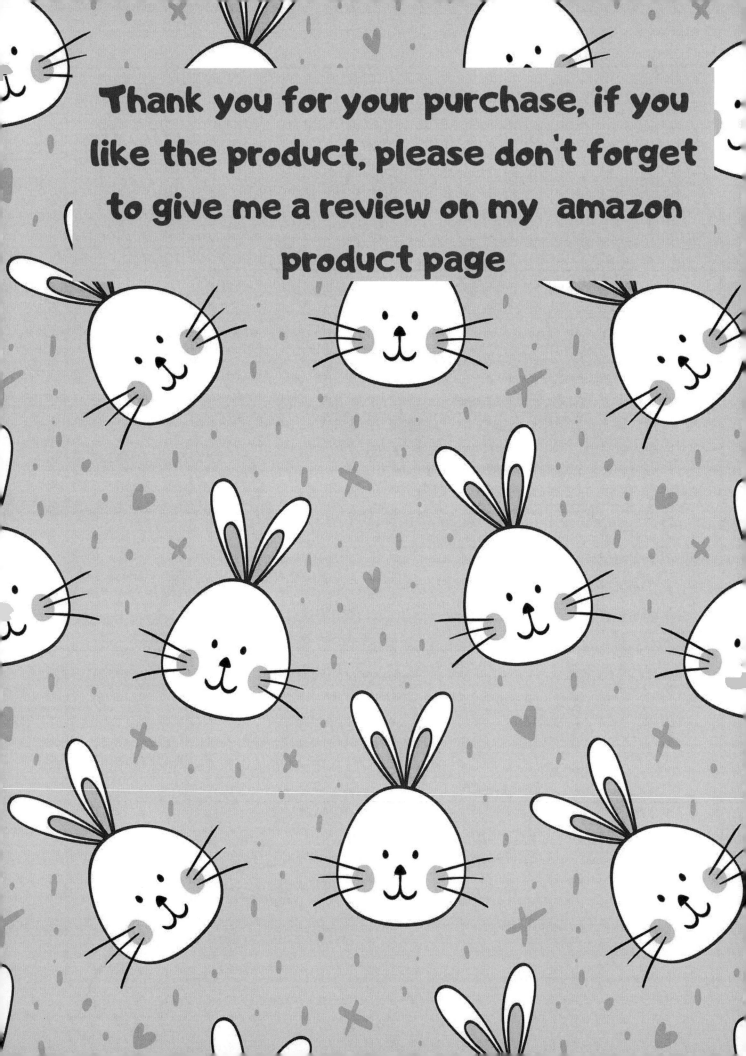

Thank you for your purchase, if you like the product, please don't forget to give me a review on my amazon product page

Made in the USA
Monee, IL
11 January 2022